THE AUTOIMMUNE
PLANT BASED
COOKBOOK

*Recipes to Decrease Pain, Optimize
Health, and Maximize Your Quality
of Life*

INCLUDES A 7 DAY MEAL PLAN!

MERCY BALLARD, RN
JOYCE CHOE, MD, MPH

Published by Wholeness for Life Publications

First paperback edition March 2019

Book design by Anointing Productions

Photography by Elizabeth Hite Photography

ISBN 978-1-7336566-0-3

www.autoimmuneplantbased.com

A Free Gift for You

We are so excited that you chose to purchase our cookbook! We have prepared a free video tutorial that will take you step-by-step through our gluten and grain-free tortilla recipe on page 97. This recipe wins hearts wherever we go, and we want to share it with you. It's our way of saying THANK YOU for purchasing our book.

Go to autoimmuneplantbased.com/tortillafreegift to watch the video tutorial.
The password: tortilla.

ACKNOWLEDGEMENTS

This book was made possible by:

Rochelle Mekowulu, thank you for pushing us to set dates and to go for them.
Elizabeth Hite, thank you for your beautiful work and all your creativity.
Nathan Hyde, thank you for your research and time.
Elizabeth Chung and Grace Chung, thank you for your feedback and encouragement.
Denise Buglino, thank you for helping Mercy with checking the recipes for accuracy.

Thank you to Lizette Balsdon (the Editing Queen) for your early work with our document and to Heidi Wallenborn (Pomegranate Creative Services) for editing our document at the very end.

Thank you to our formatter, Jesus Cordero, at Anointing Productions, who bore long and patiently with us.

We are grateful to you and to:
God for bringing blessings despite difficult circumstances
Our families for loving, encouraging, and bearing patiently with us

DISCLAIMER

We provide no warranty for the content of the recipes in our book. The recipes presented are intended for informational purposes only and we give the reader the responsibility of determining the value, quality, and nutritional value of the recipes provided.

The information provided in this book is not medical advice; it is based on our own research and understanding. Our intention is to educate our readers, but we make no claims to be able to diagnose, treat, cure, or prevent disease. We recommend that you work with your health care providers and use your own judgment before altering your diet.

TABLE OF CONTENTS

INTRODUCTION

Writing a cookbook is probably the last thing I ever thought that I would do. But then again, I've only known Mercy Ballard for the last few years. I met Mercy in January 2016 when I went to her lifestyle center, Years Restored. Watching how Mercy helped to change the lives of so many people, I was reminded of the healthcare that I had thought that I would pursue back when I was a young (and naïve) premed student. Unfortunately, I lost my way for a bit. Between the busyness of training and my focus on learning ophthalmology, I was not able to learn how to implement lifestyle medicine into my practice.

When I completed my ophthalmology training and began working in private practice, I was finally able to recollect myself and go back to my roots. I revisited the Adventist heritage that had inspired me when I was a child. Early Adventist physicians believed in the importance of educating patients about the laws of human physiology and using simple and safe methods to treat disease. I had learned some of these methods from my mother, an Adventist nurse. As I began using hydrotherapy and other simple remedies in earnest, I was gratified to see how well they worked. I also began to regularly attend medical conferences about lifestyle medicine and nutrition. I constantly armed myself with new information and looked for ways to inspire patients to live their healthiest lives. God worked through my humble efforts, and many of my patients did make significant changes. Despite the brevity of our interactions, many began to eat healthier, some lost significant amounts of weight, and some were even able to overcome addictions to cigarettes and alcohol.

It was a most humbling thing when I began to experience my own health issues. I had been helping others to get better through simple lifestyle changes; why was the lifestyle that I followed not helping me? My diet became increasingly less processed and more organic; and yet I felt weaker and experienced more pain. As I researched different lifestyles that health care providers recommended, I saw that there were many different theories and protocols, but one philosophy kept recurring: the paleo diet.

The paleo diet is based upon the philosophy that evolving humans ate a hunter/gatherer type of diet consisting of meat, vegetables, and some fruits. According to this philosophy, farming is something that only recent human civilizations have done. Grains and beans are farmed foods, so they would not have been eaten by the early evolving human. According to the paleo philosophy, these foods are harmful for even current human consumption because our digestive systems did not evolve to eat them.

Despite my belief that God was indeed Creator of the world and universe, I must admit that as I read the glowing accounts of people praising the benefits of paleo, I was very tempted to try it out for myself. However, after much study and prayer, I realized that it was not something that I could do without sacrificing my core beliefs. God had given me back my life years before when going through another crisis, and I could not support a philosophy that was based on the premise that He did not exist. I became intentional about researching my condition, what type of diet would contribute to my inflammation, and what type of a plant-based diet would help me recover.

Mercy had been on a similar path and ended up at the same conclusion years before me. She had tirelessly researched her condition, persisted in finding solutions, and now had found her lifework in helping others who still struggled. Many of her clients had advanced diseases and had tried many other options before coming to her. With each encounter, she gained valuable knowledge and expertise. Attending the program at Years Restored was something that greatly accelerated my recovery and my understanding about my condition. Mercy was able to help me close some gaps in my understanding about my disease and how to get better.

In Mercy, I found a supportive and knowledgeable mentor, and in me she found an encouraging friend. We found that we both had the desire to help more people than what we were able to do by working individually. This cookbook is one of our first collaborative efforts, and I hope that it is the first of many more things to come.

OUR JOURNEY

Mercy

You don't know what you have until it's gone...I know the meaning of these words very well. I graduated from medical school in Mexico and worked as a nurse in the United States for over two decades, but nothing prepared me for my journey with fatigue and shortness of breath that started in 2004.

Naturally athletic and energetic, I experienced progressive weakness and shortness of breath to the point that I needed hospitalization. I was diagnosed with severe anemia, received a blood transfusion and later an iron transfusion; however, the treatments helped only temporarily. As my weakness progressed, any exertion became extremely fatiguing. For two years, while I forced myself to work, most of my time at home was spent in bed.

When I realized that my healthcare providers were unable to provide a diagnosis, I persisted in researching alternative laboratory tests and therapies. Providentially, I found a lab that tested me for food sensitivities; I discovered that I had developed antibodies to gluten and other foods. I made appropriate changes in my diet and lifestyle that brought remission from arthritis, anemia, and the fatigue that had developed.

In 2013, my husband and I started a lifestyle center in central California called Years Restored. Here, we help others with chronic disease by teaching them how their diet and lifestyle can impact their health. We have seen how making simple changes can help even those with very serious autoimmune conditions turn the corner and begin to thrive. The recipes in this cookbook have been developed by learning how to cook to help myself and others with these conditions.

Our clients at the Years Restored Lifestyle Center have been blessed with incredible outcomes. It is our prayer that this information will bring physical, mental, and spiritual health to you, our reader.

Joyce

I had issues with chronic pain since my late teens due to various injuries. In 1998, after being prescribed a fluoroquinolone antibiotic called Trovafloxacin, the level of pain intensified and I developed generalized weakness that progressed over time. Trovafloxacin was shortly taken off the market due to risks of liver toxicity.

Fluoroquinolones now have a black box warning due to their many side effects. They are known to affect the mitochondria (the cellular energy producers) and connective tissue. In my case, due to my progressive weakness, I developed compression of the nerves to my right arm (thoracic outlet), pain due to repeated herniated disks, and a tendency to injure with the mildest of physical activity. At times, my entire body ached as if I had the flu; I found it difficult to think clearly.

In 2011, pain intensified and began affecting my hands and wrists. With my livelihood threatened, I redoubled my efforts to find a solution for my problem. I was referred to a functional medicine healthcare provider who diagnosed me with leaky gut.

As I followed a plant-based elimination diet and learned how to detox, my symptoms slowly improved. Yet in 2015 when I reintroduced soy, corn, and wheat back into my diet they slowly returned. In addition to arthritic and muscular pain, I developed shortness of breath, allergic symptoms, and chronic sinus congestion. I found the courage to share these issues with a few doctors—they either manifested skepticism when I told them about my symptoms, or—despite sympathy—could provide no answers. I was told by pulmonologists that my abnormal lung function studies were normal because I was "a small, Asian woman," and there was nothing more to do. I resigned myself to a slow downward spiral.

It can be very isolating and emotionally overwhelming to have food sensitivities. Your friends, family, and doctors may be skeptical about whether leaky gut and food intolerance are true medical conditions, and some may feel that your symptoms are all in your head. Believing in the benefits of a totally plant-based diet made it even more isolating for me. Most of my alternative healthcare providers did not support a total plant-based approach, and I felt pressure to adopt a "paleo" diet and lifestyle.

Most of the people around me probably thought that I was an extreme health nut because of how careful I was with my diet. I didn't look unwell, I never missed work, and I maintained a positive attitude. All the while, I looked for ways to minimize pain, to stay off of medications, and to avoid becoming disabled. Looking back, I can see that as difficult as it was to feel misunderstood, these experiences ultimately helped me to grow, to learn patience, and to learn to trust in God through each difficulty.

In January 2016, I went to the Years Restored 10-day detox program. On the third day of the program, I realized that I no longer felt the pain with which I had come to the program. The shortness of breath was also gone. I remember thinking, *This must be what it feels like to be normal.* Thus began the next chapter of my life.

When you are just starting out on this journey, it can be extremely confusing. There is a plethora of research in the scientific world and there are numerous contradictory opinions about what is the most anti-inflammatory diet and lifestyle. I believe that a loving God has given us principles in His Word that can shed light on even this confusing subject. That God would not leave us "in the dark" is the framework that Mercy and I had as we searched for answers that were supported by Biblical principles, scientific research, and clinical experience.

We can share with confidence that even for autoimmune disease and leaky gut, lifestyle and diet can have a huge impact. Many who have tried this plant based approach—even as a last resort— have made significant improvement. While each individual has different food sensitivities and the recipes may need to be tweaked, the principles do work. We hope that this book will help you in your journey toward health and to a deeper appreciation about how we are fearfully and wonderfully made.

WHO THIS IS FOR

While these recipes are specifically designed to help those with leaky gut, food sensitivities, and autoimmune disease, we believe that this cookbook will be helpful for anyone interested in decreasing inflammation and improving their quality of life. It is actually a misconception that leaky gut manifests only with digestive issues. Most of us have been affected by gut permeability to one degree or another. Consider the possibility of leaky gut if you have been diagnosed with any disease or if you experience debilitating symptoms such as: fatigue, brain fog, pain, weakness, bloating, constipation, diarrhea, depression, anxiety, and eczema. Do any of these describe you? We want to help!

PART I

GETTING INFORMED

AUTOIMMUNE DISEASE

Autoimmune disease is one of the most common chronic conditions affecting Americans, and the incidence is rising. According to officials with the American Autoimmune Related Diseases Association, about 20 percent of the population—or 50 million Americans—have an autoimmune condition.[1] This is a condition where your body's defense system—the immune system—loses its ability to recognize its own cells and starts attacking healthy cells as it would a bacterial or viral invader. Common examples of autoimmune diseases include Hashimoto's thyroiditis, lupus, Sjogren's disease, psoriasis, rheumatoid arthritis, and multiple sclerosis. The immune system can attack any system or organ in the body; according to some estimates, there are upwards of eighty different types of autoimmune diseases.[2] Treatment options are quite limited as steroids, immune system suppressing drugs, and pain medications all have devastating side effects.

The Immune System—Defense, Repair, and Waste Management

Antibodies are proteins produced by the immune system to help remove pathogens. They are what we use to fight infections and even cancer. Autoantibodies are proteins that are produced against self. One function they serve is to remove cells that are injured or dead. This serves as a kind of sanitation system that removes waste that would otherwise accumulate around our cells.

Have you ever wondered what would cause your body to become so confused that it would turn against itself and produce pathogenic autoantibodies? A genetic predisposition does play a role. But in the majority of chronic diseases, whether or not these genes turn on or off is determined by lifestyle choices that we make.[3]

Here are some causes of cell injury and death—triggers for a condition that we call **inflammation.**

1. Infections—Having a weak immune system makes one vulnerable to harboring disease-causing viruses, bacteria and fungi.[4]

2. Toxins, mold, pesticides,[5] plastics,[6] heavy metals,[7] hair dyes,[8] cosmetics and body care ingredients.[9]

3. Pharmaceutical drugs, vaccines,[10] oral contraceptives,[11] hormone replacement therapy.[12]

4. Nutrition—sugar,[13] refined carbohydrates,[14] flavor enhancers,[15] aroma enhancers, preservatives, emulsifiers,[16] thickeners, vinegars, and pickled foods are just some of the things that may contribute to inflammation.

5. Stress[17]—emotional, physical, mental. This can be known or even subconscious. Bitterness, resentment, and a lack of forgiveness can cause stress to consume our resources. Depression itself is a known risk factor for disease.[18]

6. Lifestyle practices—lack of sleep,[19] lack of exercise,[20] lack of sunlight,[21] lack of fresh air.[22]

The more sources of inflammation you are exposed to and the longer you are exposed to them, the more you will have to take from your reserve of immune cells. These are cells that would otherwise be available for the routine maintenance and surveillance. Over time, the choices that lead to inflammation will result in more confusion and chaos for the immune system, thus the scene is set for disease, dysfunction, and degeneration.

Diseases of the Immune System and the Gut

In recent decades, there has been a significant upsurge in diseases involving the immune system, such as allergies, cancer, and autoimmune disease. While the exact reason for this trend may not be readily identified, the gut may be a good place to begin looking, since the major part of the immune system resides there.

Seventy to eighty percent of the body's immune cells are located in the digestive system. In addition to providing immune cells, the lining of the gut—the *epithelium*—is a very important protective structure, because this is where digestion and absorption of food takes place and where the *microbiome*—the bacteria, viruses, fungi, and protozoa—live.

The microbiome contains about ten times as many cells as the rest of the human body and is absolutely essential for good digestion, physical strength, healthy emotions, and a balanced immune function.[23]

In autoimmune disease (as well as in many other chronic diseases) the gut microbiome has been significantly altered and exists in a state of imbalance, or "dysbiosis." Not surprisingly, there is a distinct correlation between the health of the gut microbiome and the development of autoimmune diseases.[24-27]

The gut epithelium is made up of a *single layer* of epithelial cells. These cells are protected by a layer of **mucus** and interlocked by structures called *tight junctions*. All of these provide a protective barrier to pathogens and undigested food particles. It is the breakdown of this barrier that allows pathogens or incompletely digested food molecules to enter into the body.

This condition of *gut permeability* is called *"leaky gut,"* a condition associated with sensitivities to various foods. These sensitivities can manifest with a wide variety of symptoms including pain, allergies, eczema, fatigue, and brain fog. Gut permeability can contribute to many diseases, including the different types of autoimmune diseases we see today.[28, 29]

If you have leaky gut, you may not even be able to tolerate foods that are supposed to be good for you, such as onions, garlic, or even greens. This is most likely due to the dysbiosis that has developed when beneficial bacteria required for proper digestion are outnumbered by opportunistic and harmful bacteria that colonize the digestive system instead. The good news is that you can repopulate your gut with the correct bacteria. Just as the gut microbiome can change with negative lifestyle choices, it responds favorably to a modification of lifestyle, especially the diet.

THE GLUTEN FACTOR

Gluten has an effect on our health through various mechanisms. It can overstimulate the immune system, create toxic reactions, and negatively affect the microbiome composition. The resulting dysbiosis (imbalance of the various types of bacteria) will further contribute to intestinal permeability.[30,31,32] This gluten-induced gut permeability is an issue for celiac disease patients, as well as for those who are simply gluten sensitive.[30]

There are a number of possible reasons for why gluten sensitivity is such an issue today. One explanation may be the hybridization of wheat, which may cause the modern varieties of wheat to be more difficult to digest than the varieties grown a century ago.[33]

Another reason may be the effect that industrialized food production has had on our digestive systems. A commonly used agricultural practice is that of mono-cropping, or the intensive planting of the same one crop on the same large piece of land. This is a commonly used practice that imbalances the soil and requires intensive pesticide use. Food that is grown from this poor soil lacks severely in nutrition and the overall vitality needed for human health.[34,35]

Roundup® is one of the most widely used herbicides. It is routinely used on many grain crops (including wheat), legumes, and many vegetables. Glyphosate, the active ingredient in Roundup®, has been patented as a mineral chelator, antibiotic, and herbicide. Because it did not cause acute toxicity and because humans lack the shikimate pathway that glyphosate affects, it was quickly pronounced to be safe when it came on the market in the 1970s.[36] Various independent studies have since demonstrated that it may negatively impact various cellular enzymes. Glyphosate may indeed be one of the most important factors in the gluten epidemic.[37,38]

THE 3 R'S OF EATING TO HEAL

The 3 R's

R1

Remove inflammatory foods that feed bad bacteria and increase the risk of leaky gut. Foods that are most commonly associated with food sensitivities include: gluten, soy, corn, eggs, dairy, and yeast. We are also seeing oats more commonly appearing on the list of food sensitivities. If you test positive for these foods, we recommend that you not reintroduce them back into the diet, even after the gut has healed.

Meat and dairy products are sources of inflammation in a number of ways. They provide saturated fats which are sources for the building blocks of inflammatory

15

mediators, they bio-amplify (or concentrate) pesticides and toxins taken in from the environment, and they are also sources of lipopolysaccharide, a potent inflammatory toxin.

Grains and nuts may not be well-tolerated early on in the healing process; one should wait until the gut is healed to incorporate these foods into the diet. Nightshade plants, such as potatoes, tomatoes, eggplants and peppers may also cause symptoms for many, however, they may be better tolerated after the gut has healed.

Nutritional yeast is a very popular product among vegetarians, however, both nutritional and baker's yeast are associated with an inflammatory bowel condition called Crohn's disease and tend to be poorly tolerated in those with gut permeability issues.[39] Whether it is because the media that the yeast is grown upon is usually from genetically modified corn or from wheat treated with glyphosate—the reason for this intolerance is not known. At this point we do not use yeast in any of our recipes.

One quick way to discover foods that are causing inflammation is to test for food sensitivities. Serum testing can be helpful for some and may be covered by certain insurance companies. Another way to discover food sensitivities is to eliminate foods that are most commonly associated with food sensitivities and to reintroduce them one at a time after the gut has healed. This process will take much longer and may not reveal as much as food sensitivity testing would. We have personally found that stool testing by Enterolab may be one of the most sensitive ways to detect food sensitivities, however, we recommend that one try various methods of testing as there is no one particular test that will provide all answers for all individuals.

R2

Replace harmful with helpful food. The following are principles for repopulating the gut with good bacteria:

Eat from a variety of raw plant foods. A large portion (we recommend about 70%) of your diet should be raw. This will help to repopulate the gut with the diverse microbial life that it should have.[40] The meal plan in our book will help give you an idea of how to put a meal together. You will see that leafy green and other colored vegetables are included daily. Other things to eat every day include: garlic and onions, steamed cruciferous vegetables (lightly steamed to decrease goitrogenic effects), seeds (for omega-3 and other fats, proteins, vitamins, and minerals), and berries (high in fiber and antioxidants)

Eat organic foods that have not been grown with harmful pesticides or genetically modified organisms (GMO). We prepare most of our own food from fresh or frozen organic sources and avoid canned and prepackaged foods. Canned foods are not as healthy as other types of foods, not only because of the heat used, but also because of the metal, plastic, and BPA exposure. Processed and boxed foods typically have preservatives and additives that are detrimental to gut and microbiome health. Glyphosate, one of the most commonly used pesticides, is an antibiotic and a mineral chelator which can be found in many foods. It will destroy gut bacteria and bind to important minerals—which has significant health consequences. Unfortunately, it is used on many crops; significant concentrations can be found in numerous prepackaged foods that many consider to be healthy and "natural."[41]

Eat a diet that is high in fiber; it is what beneficial gut bacteria feed on and therefore plays an important role in promoting good bacteria.[42] Only plant sources of food will have fiber.

We do not recommend immune-stimulating plants and herbs such as chlorella, spirulina, echinacea, and alfalfa. Immune-stimulating foods can increase the risk of autoimmune disease.[43-45]

To provide the best source of nutrition for health-promoting bacteria, avoid animal products and eat a whole-food plant-based diet from organic sources.[46,47] Animal products such as meat, eggs, and dairy, may have some healthful properties, but the overall effect will be inflammatory. A number of factors contribute to this inflammation including: bioamplification of pesticides and toxins, colonization with disease causing viruses, the high lipopolysaccharide content of animal products (a powerful endotoxin that is heat resistant and will not be cooked out), and saturated fat content which increases arachidonic acid and inflammatory mediators.[48, 49]

Avoid free fats. Polyunsaturated fats are very healthy, yet when they are extracted from their food source, the free fat become vulnerable to the effects of light, air, moisture and heat on their double bond structures. We use foods such as avocados, seeds, coconuts, and nuts to add fats to the diet without using free extracted fats.

R3

Repair the digestive system with healthy superfoods, fasting, and natural remedies. In addition to the diet, various superfoods such as turmeric, garlic, carob, maca, and dried herbs can be helpful to aid healing. Natural remedies such as hydrotherapy, poultices, and enemas may also be helpful.

Keep in mind that it is not only what you eat but how you eat that influences health. Regular meal times, eating smaller amounts, not drinking liquids with your meals, and avoiding certain food combinations are all simple changes that will yield large benefits.

Fasting helps to reset the digestive system and decrease inflammatory mediators. We recommend that the third meal of your day be very light, and better yet, not be eaten at all. This will provide a daily intermittent fast that will greatly speed your recovery. For this reason, our 7-day meal plan provides recipes for only breakfast and lunch.

PHASES OF HEALING

Phase 1: This book is designed to assist you through the critical initial phase of gut restoration, which will take approximately two months for mild cases and four months (or longer) for more serious cases. In this stage:

1. Grains and nuts are avoided, since these foods are difficult to digest.

2. Pseudograins such as quinoa, amaranth and buckwheat are used instead of grains.

3. Seeds such as pumpkin and sunflower are used instead of nuts.

Phase 2: When your leaky gut is restored to health, you can start reintroducing grains, nuts, and other foods on your food sensitivity list, one by one. Wait a few days between each reintroduced food to see if there are any reactions. However, if you tested positively for sensitivity to gluten, soy, corn, yeast, or oats, we recommend that these in particular not be reintroduced. You may attempt to reintroduce other grains such as sorghum, millet, teff, and rice after symptoms subside.

PART II

GETTING PREPARED

HOW TO REMOVE ANTINUTRIENTS

Antinutrients are compounds that can interfere with nutrient absorption. Major sources of antinutrients include grains, seeds, nuts, and legumes. Some not only interfere with nutrient absorption, but bind to the intestinal wall and cause intestinal inflammation as well.[50,51] Soaking, sprouting, and cooking are all processes that will decrease antinutrient content and increase nutrient availability and digestibility.[52]

Soaking

In general, we recommend soaking grains, seeds, nuts and legumes at least overnight. Longer soak times and frequent rinses during the soaking process will decrease antinutrient content in the food.

A general rule of thumb is to soak one to three cups of the selected grain, seed, nut, or legume overnight in a large glass jar or bowl. Cover with at least triple the amount of water. Soak for 12 hours and rinse well.

Grains and nuts

To help with the healing process, AVOID grains and nuts for the first few months of your recovery process. Our recipes do not include any grains and nuts. We recommend that when you do reintroduce them, soak overnight before ingesting or processing.

Legumes

SOAK legumes overnight in pure water before use. Certain legumes are better tolerated than others. Kidney and navy beans have antinutrients that can be difficult to tolerate; soaking longer (24-72 hours) with more frequent rinses (at least twice a day) during the soaking process will help decrease the antinutrient content even further.

Pumpkin and Sunflower Seeds

Fatty seeds—such as pumpkin and sunflower seeds—are used in a large number of our recipes. They can be stored in the freezer in their native state and soaked overnight before use. Or, if planning to use the seeds to make seed butters, the soaked and rinsed seeds should be dehydrated for 24 hours. They can be stored in the freezer so that you can have them on hand whenever you need to make the butters.

Chia and flax seed

Soaking may improve digestibility for these seeds. A rule of thumb for soaking these seeds is to place 1 tablespoon of seed in 3 tablespoons of water. You would then use the water/seed mixture because it would be too viscous to rinse.

Pseudograins

Amaranth, quinoa, and buckwheat are plant seeds known as **"pseudograins,"** because they can often be used in place of grains. They have a different nutritional and mineral profile than the grains they substitute because they are not the grass seeds (as grains are), but of broad, leafy plants. Pseudograins tend to be better tolerated by the digestive system than grains are. However, they still contain antinutrients and do need to be soaked overnight. Thoroughly rinse your seeds before using.

Sprouting

Sprouting helps to further decrease antinutrients and will even increase the nutrient availability of soaked food. Certain seeds and legumes are easier to sprout than others. Pseudograins such as amaranth and buckwheat sprout very easily and can be sprouted for a couple of days before use. We have found that quinoa begins to smell "sour" if it is sprouted longer than a day or two.

It is fun to make flours with sprouted pseudograins to use for baking. To make flours, the sprouts need to be dry. We recommend you soak, sprout, and dehydrate larger amounts of pseudograins that can be stored in an airtight container in the freezer. To process into a flour, use a mill or a high-speed blender. Sprouted flours can also be purchased from online sources.

Sprouting seeds

Use 1 tablespoon of broccoli, radish, or other seeds. Soak the seeds in a 16 oz canning jar overnight with at least 2-3x the amount of water. Rinse after soaking and drain all the fluid. Use a sprouting lid and place jar upside down at an angle so that water can drain out entirely and air can freely enter. Keep the jar in the dark until sprouts develop. Then place it by a window with sun exposure. Rinse at least twice a day. It will take 5 to 7 days until fully sprouted. Use on sandwiches, salads and wraps, etc.

Chia and Flax seed—the seeds with higher levels of omega 3 fats—are difficult to sprout. Our recipes use these in both raw and cooked form and do not call for sprouting. Our recipes do not call for sprouted sunflower or pumpkin seeds.

Sprouting buckwheat

Soak 3 cups of raw hulled buckwheat overnight in a 64-ounce wide-mouth glass jar. Rinse several times until the liquid becomes clear. It will take many rinses because the fluid is rather viscous. Cover the jar with a sprouting lid and keep it tilted downward at an angle so that air can still enter and fluid can entirely drain. Keep the jar in a dark area until sprouts develop. You should see small sprouts develop after a day. Rinse morning and evening, for a total of two days (do not sprout for more than three days).

Sprouting quinoa

Soak 3 cups quinoa overnight in a 2-pint canning glass container. Rinse enough times that the liquid becomes clear. Cover the jar with a sprouting lid and place it upside down at an angle so that air can still enter and fluid can drain entirely. Keep in darkness until sprouts develop—due to the small size of the seeds, it may be difficult to see the sprout). Rinse sprouts morning and evening until you are ready to use. Do not sprout for more than one to two days. We dehydrate sprouted quinoa and use it to make flour for baking.

Cooking

Cooking pseudograins

Pseudograins do not require as much cooking time as grains. Soak pseudograins overnight, rinse and then cook for 15-30 minutes.

Cooking legumes:

Our practice is to soak legumes overnight and to rinse well the following day. Cooking beans usually takes about an hour; the time varies with the type of bean. **Avoid adding salt until the legumes are almost done cooking;** salt will prevent the bean from softening while it cooks.

Lentils, mung, lima, and garbanzo beans are varieties which can be cooked after soaking overnight. Kidney and navy beans contain a sugar for which the body does not carry the enzyme to digest. Some recommend that these beans be soaked for one to three days, rinsing twice per day and refilling with fresh water.

Those who have difficulty tolerating beans can further decrease the antinutrient content by rinsing the legumes during the cooking process. Bring the legumes to a boil and rinse; add water, the seasonings (other than salt) and bring to a second boil. Lower the heat and simmer the legumes for at least an hour.

Another method to cook the beans is to use a slow-cooker for up to a couple days.

Raw or cooked?

Grains and legumes require longer cooking times to adequately break down or hydrolyze the starches and to avoid inflammation. For this reason, we do not recommend that grains or legumes ever be eaten raw, even after soaking overnight (as in the case of overnight oats!).

While buckwheat seems to be well-tolerated eaten raw after sprouting, we are not sure about how digestible raw amaranth and quinoa are even after sprouting; we recommend that these be further processed by cooking or baking to improve digestibility. Chia and flax seeds can be used in raw form and may be more digestible after soaking.

PREPARING PSEUDOGRAINS

Product	Soak Time	Cereal:Water*	Cook Time	Comments
Amaranth	8-12 hours	1:2-1:3	**Stove** 20-30 minutes Crockpot - 8 hr or overnight	Dry thoroughly to store/ eat as cereal
Buckwheat	6-12 hours	1:1-1:2	**Stove** 15-20 minutes, or until cooked thoroughly **Bake** - per recipe **Crock Pot** - overnight **Dehydrate** - per recipe	Buy raw, hulled buckwheat, not the roasted groats (Kasha). Water will be very viscous after soaking overnight. **Rinse** very well before sprouting. **Rinse** twice a day for 2-3 days of sprouting. **Rinse** when done soaking and sprouting.
Quinoa	8-12 hours	1:1-1:2	15 min (or until they are cooked completely)	Dehydrate thoroughly to store.

* Cereal to Water Ratio when Cooking

USING SEEDS

Product	Soak Time	Comments
Chia Seed	Few hours	Cannot rinse due to viscous fluid
Flax Seed	Few hours	Cannot rinse due to viscous fluid
Pumpkin Seed	8-10 hours	Dehydrate thoroughly to store
Sunflower Seed	8-10 hours	Dehydrate thoroughly to store

COOKING LEGUMES

Product	Soak Time	Legume:Water*	Cook Time	Comments
Beans- Black, Pinto, Red, White, Etc.	12-24 hours, change water x 2	1:4	Stove: 1 to 2 hrs. until soft Crockpot: 8 hrs	Remove foam while cooking. Add salt near end of cook time.
Chickpeas (Garbanzo)	12-24 hours, change water x 2	1:4	Stove: 1 to 2 hrs. until soft Crockpot: 8 hrs	Add salt near end of cook time.
Fava Beans	8-12 hours	1:4	Stove 1 hr. until soft Crockpot: 8 hrs	Add salt near end of cook time.

*Legume to water ratio for soaking and cooking

Lentils, Brown, Green, Red	8-12 hours	1:2	Stove: 30-40 min. until soft	Add salt near end of cook time. Red lentils cook faster than green/brown
Lima Beans	8-12 hours	1:4	Stove: 1 - 2 hrs. Crockpot: 8 hours	Add salt near end of cook time.
Mung Beans	8-12 hours	1:3	Stove: 30 - 40 min, until soft	Add salt near end of cook time.

STOCKING THE PANTRY

The availability of ingredients will vary, depending on your location. In general, pseudograins (amaranth, buckwheat, and quinoa) and seeds (flax, chia, sunflower, and pumpkin) can usually be purchased from the bulk section at most grocery stores in urban areas.

Both young and mature coconuts can be purchased online as well as from local health or Asian grocery stores. Young coconuts appear white because their outer yellow/green skin has been removed and the white fleshy husk remains. They should be fairly white and fresh in appearance. Young coconuts have a sweet liquid inside that many will drink as "coconut water" or blend with the meat to make coconut milk. Mature coconuts have lost the fleshy white husks and only the very tough brown shell remains. The water inside a mature coconut will not be used in any recipes, however, there is much more meat, which can be used to blend with water to make coconut milk.

All legumes, pseudograins, omega-3 seeds, leafy green vegetables, roots (garlic, onion, potatoes, sweet potatoes, etc.), fruits with edible and/or thin skin (berries, apples, kiwis, etc.) should always be from organic sources. It is also helpful for fruits with thicker peels (avocados, lemons, grapefruits, coconuts, etc.) to be from organic sources.

If they are not available from local sources, recipe items can easily be purchased from online sources that offer non-GMO, organic, and earth-conscious products at affordable prices. Consider purchasing bulk quantities for cost-effectiveness, and check autoimmuneplantbased. com or drjoycechoe.com for online resource recommendations.

STORAGE TIPS

Leftover cooked legumes or cereals can be stored in the refrigerator for up to three to five days. Leftover liquids such as coconut and sunflower seed milk should be stored for no longer than three days. Leftover butters such as pumpkin seed or sunflower seed butter can be stored in the refrigerator for a week or two. Seed butters can be stored in the freezer if they are not going to be used right away, and taste great even after defrosting. We recommend storing foods in glass containers, to avoid BPA or other toxin exposures.

Pseudograins can be stored for long term storage in sealed containers at room temperature—after they are soaked overnight and dehydrated. If dehydrated and ground into a flour, they can either be stored in the refrigerator for short term usage, or stored in the freezer if they will not be used for a while. Dried beans and dried pseudograins can be kept in sealed containers for long term storage.

For meal planning purposes, we recommend that you prepare larger amounts of beans, pseudograins, waffles, and breads and store them in the freezer to have on hand when you are too busy to make them from scratch.

EQUIPMENT

It is vital to have the correct tools to prepare the foods. You will find the following to be handy.

High-speed blender

A high-speed blender is essential for daily smoothies, creams, sauces, gravies, milks, and pesto sauces, and will save time and money. We would recommend that you also purchase a dry container to make flours from your sprouted seeds. This does not need to be done right away.

Food Processor

A food processor will speed up the time it takes to chop, slice, and shred. Salsas and other vegetable toppings can be made in just minutes. It's also handy to make raw crackers, gluten-free pizza crusts, dough for flatbreads and tortillas, and butters from seeds and nuts. We recommend a 13-cup food processor for these recipes.

Dehydrator

Dehydrators allow you to preserve foods for long-term storage and convenience. Granola, crackers, chips, pizza crust, and fruit leathers can all be made very quickly and conveniently with the aid of a dehydrator. The dehydration process is also economical in helping make spreadable butters out of seeds and nuts which are soaked first and then dehydrated, before being processed into butters.

Directions for seeds: Soak large quantities of seeds overnight and rinse well. Cut parchment paper to appropriate size to cover each tray. Place thin layer of seeds over the parchment paper. Dehydrate for 24 hours or until dry. Store in airtight container in freezer for future recipes.

Other Kitchen Tools

Waffle iron

A good waffle iron is necessary for our buckwheat waffle recipe. If you don't have an iron, you can use the recipe for pancakes instead.

Spiralizer

Spiralizers can make raw noodles out of vegetables such as zucchini. These can be topped with pesto or plant-based cheese or cream.

Lemon Squeezer

We use a lot of lemons! A squeezer will save time and effort.

Coconut tool

There are coconut tools that help open coconuts, and tools to help harvest the meat inside. We use a large knife to open the young coconuts and the back of a spoon to harvest the meat.

Nut milk bag

Blending seeds or nuts with water to make milk will result in a liquid mixture containing much pulp. A nut milk bag allows you to easily separate milk from pulp, which can be saved and used for other recipes.

Double ended spatula

We highly recommended smaller sized double-ended spatulas to help spread doughs and crackers.

Dehydrator templates for raw foods

Rawsome Creations is one source of templates. These templates make it easy to have perfectly circular wraps and crackers every time!

Tortilla Press

If you are someone who enjoys tortillas, this will be something that you will want to purchase. We have an excellent tortilla recipe!

SHOPPING LIST FOR THE 7-DAY MEALPLAN

Miscellaneous	Seasoning	Fruits and Vegetables
Agar powder	Cardamom	Apple (Granny Smith)
Arrowroot	Cayenne pepper	Avocado
Buckwheat	Coriander	Basil
Carob powder, brown	Cumin	Bell pepper
Carob powder, white (Australian)	Dill	Berries (all kinds)
Chia Seed	Garlic powder	Broccoli
Coconut, shredded	Marjoram	Carrot
Flaxseed, golden	Onion powder	Celery
Guar gum	Oregano	Cilantro
Honey, raw	Paprika	Cauliflower
Pumpkin seed	Parsley	Coconut, brown
Stevia	Sage	Coconut, young
Salt	thyme	Cucumber
Sunflower seed		Garlic
Vanilla bean		Green Onion

Legumes	Pseudograins	
Garbanzo	Amaranth	Kiwi
Kidney	Buckwheat	Lemon
Lentil, brown	Quinoa	Onion
Lentil, red		Olive
Mung bean		Parsley
Lima bean		Pomegranate
Pinto bean		Potato
		Tomato
		Spinach
		Sweet Potato, Asian
		Yuca
		Zucchini

DAILY SERVINGS FOR THE AUTOIMMUNE PLANT BASED PROTOCOL

Food Group	Servings	Serving Amount
Berries	1	1/2 cup fresh
Other fruits	5	1 cup fresh
Omega 3: Flaxseed, chia seed, walnut, purslane	1	1-2 tablespoons
Whole grains and Pseudograins: Whole grains: Millet, rice, sorghum, teff, (oats and corn ok if food sensitivity test is negative) Pseudograins: Buckwheat, quinoa, amaranth	3	1/2 cup cereal, 1 tortilla, 1 slice of bread
Nuts and Fatty seeds Nuts: Almonds, cashews, brazil nuts, walnuts, pine nuts, pecans, macadamia and fatty seeds Fatty acid seeds: Sunflower seeds, pumpkin seeds	1	1/4 cup, 2 table-spoons seed butters
Legumes: Pinto, kidney, black, navy beans, black eyed peas, garbanzo, lentils, lima beans	3	1/2 cup cooked legumes, 1/4 cup hummus
Cruciferous: Broccoli, chards, cabbage, collard, kale, garden cress, bok choy, cauliflower, mustard greens	1	1/2 cup
Greens: Lettuce, arugula, dandelion, spinach, parsley, cilantro, green onion, leeks, celery	2	1 cup minimum
Other vegetables: Zucchini, potatoes, sweet potatoes, tomatoes, beets, bell peppers, cucumber, yellow squash, artichoke, okra, turnip, tomatillo	2	1/2 cup (minimum)
Spices+herbs: Turmeric + Basil, Cilantro, Oregano, Thyme, Dill, Parsley, Rosemary	1	1/2 teaspoon of turmeric + 1/2 tea-spoon dried herbs
Allium vegetables: Garlic, onion, green onion, leeks, chives	2	2 cloves garlic, 1/4 cup onions

THE 7 DAY MEAL PLAN

The 7-day meal plan is intended to be followed for the first few months as you recover from your symptoms. We rotate various foods so that you are less likely to become sensitive to any one. We have found that our clients have less confusion when they have a meal plan, rather than being given numerous recipes to choose from. For this reason, many recipes are included in the meal plan format.

Each breakfast includes a flatbread, seed butter, and smoothie. Each lunch includes a green salad. A high-speed blender is necessary; a food processor is highly recommended for the 7-day meal plan. A dehydrator is not needed for the meals, but will be necessary for some of the additional recipes. As you expand your repertoire and kitchen tools, you can use the additional recipes to supplement or take the place of the meal plan recipes.

Eating for Better Gut Health

1. Eat organic, plant-based, and high nutrient foods.

2. Eat mostly raw. We recommend 70 percent of your diet be raw.

3. Soak seeds, legumes, and pseudograins before use. Do the same for nuts and grains when they are reincorporated into the diet.

4. Don't depend upon others to meet your food needs. Do commit to preparing most of your own food, rather than eating out, because every meal counts.

5. Eat your fruits at one meal and greens at another. We eat fruits at the breakfast meal and greens at the lunch meal. This separation of fruits and vegetables makes it easier on digestion.

6. Hydrate well throughout the day with pure water.

7. Avoid drinking with your meals which may dilute stomach acid and interfere with digestion. We do not include any soup recipes in this book for the same reason. Drink water throughout the day, until fifteen minutes before meals. Wait one to two hours after meals to start drinking again.

8. Rest the gut between meals. We do not recommend any snacking between meals and we recommend that breakfast and lunch be eaten at least five hours apart. This allows the gut to rest for an hour or so before going through another digestive process.

9. Avoid hyperglycemia and hypoglycemia. Our balanced meals are designed to sustain blood sugars.

10. Make the dinner meal light. Drink an onion broth or fast. This allows the digestive system to rest through the night.

11. Chew small amounts of food slowly and thoroughly. This puts less stress on the rest of the digestive system.

12. Eat in a pleasant atmosphere. Eating in a rushed, stressful, or emotionally-charged environment will interfere with digestion.

13. Exercise before meals to help your cells work up an appetite. Go for a light ten-minute walk after meals to help with digestion and blood sugar management. Avoid strenuous exercise after eating, as this will draw circulation away from the digestive organs!

14. Avoid grains and nuts in the first 2-4 months of healing.

    • Use pseudograins in place of grains.
    • Use sunflower and pumpkin seeds in place of nuts.
    • Use flax seeds and chia seeds to help further decrease inflammation

15. Avoid dessert recipes until your gut has healed. Many people with leaky gut have candida issues and cannot tolerate the sugar content of many fruits. Better tolerated fruits include green apples, berries, kiwis, and pomegranates.

16. Don't overeat. Whether you eat too much at any one meal or eat too frequently or snack in between meals, this may be one of the most serious problems for your digestive health.

Tips for Success on Your Health Journey

1. Make a commitment to yourself to seek for better health. Give yourself time to learn and to prepare, but commit to the journey of getting better.

2. Start simple. We recommend a lot of healthy changes, so start wherever you are! You can start with something as simple as eating a beautiful organic salad every day with one of our delicious dressings! Or try soaking beans overnight. Give yourself a quick win!

3. Make progress. Try one new thing, make it your own, and then keep on learning.

4. Focus on things that make this a positive experience. The journey is as important as the destination.

5. Celebrate your wins. Make sure that your self-talk is encouraging and uplifting. Congratulate yourself for the progress you make.

6. Be your best friend and encourage yourself when you fail.

7. Trust in God. Healthy living may seem impossible for us to do, but with God, all things are possible. Matt 19:26.

PART III

RECIPES FOR THE 7 DAY MEAL PLAN

BREAKFAST **DAY 1**

Buckwheat Waffles, Carob Mousse, Pumpkin Seed Protein Power Smoothie, Flat Bread, and Seed Butter

We haven't met anyone who misses gluten when they are munching on these buckwheat waffles! Simple, easy to make, and super yummy, these are a winner.

Ingredients:

- 1 cup hulled raw buckwheat groats, soaked overnight and rinsed
- ½ cup sunflower seeds, soaked overnight and rinsed
- ½ cup arrowroot
- 1 tablespoon honey
- 2 teaspoons vanilla extract
- ½ teaspoon unrefined salt
- 1 cup water
- Top with an assortment of berries, kiwis, pomegranates, and green apples, when in season

Servings: Makes a little over three waffles
Prep time: 5-10 minutes
Cook time: 25 minutes
(3 waffles)

Directions:

1. Soak your buckwheat and sunflower seeds overnight and rinse well before using. (They will double in size. Use all)
2. Preheat the waffle iron to the highest setting
3. Place all ingredients into a high-speed blender container
4. Blend all ingredients to a smooth runny batter consistency. Assess after blending. You may need to add up to ¼ cup more water to make a thinner consistency and a runnier batter.
5. Pour the batter into the waffle iron and bake at the highest setting, until steam is no longer emitted. For our Belgian waffle iron, this takes approximately eight minutes.
6. Serve with berries, kiwis, pomegranates, cut apples and sweetener of choice.

Ingredients:

- Scoop out the meat of one young coconut. Approximately 1 cup
- 1 small avocado
- 1 tablespoon honey
- 2 tablespoons carob powder
- ½ teaspoon stevia leaf
- 1 teaspoon vanilla
- 1 cup coconut water or pure water

Servings: 2 cups
Prep time: 10 minutes

CAROB MOUSSE

It is important that you use a fresh young coconut, because it won't taste the same with dehydrated coconut flakes or a mature coconut.

Directions:

1. Blend all ingredients in a high-speed blender until very smooth.

Ingredients:

- 2 tablespoons pumpkin seeds, soaked
- 1 tablespoon flaxseed
- ½ cup berries
- 1 apple
- 2 tablespoons shredded coconut
- 2 tablespoons carob powder
- ¾ cup water

Servings: 12 ounces, one serving
Prep time: 5-10 minutes

PUMPKIN SEED PROTEIN SMOOTHIE

This smoothie tastes great without being too sweet. Many with leaky gut have candida issues and cannot tolerate fruits that are too sweet and so green apples and berries are the major sweeteners here.

Directions:

1. Blend all ingredients and serve.

Serve with flatbread and seed butter of choice (see p. 89-91).

LUNCH **DAY 1**

Lima Beans with Toppings, Cooked Yuca, Steamed Broccoli, Mixed Green Salad

The beans can be made days to weeks in advance and frozen in a meal-sized container for convenience. Remember to start soaking the beans at least 12-24 hours in advance of cooking.

Ingredients:

- 2 cups dried lima beans (large) soaked at least 8 hours and rinsed
- ½ of a medium onion
- 1 stalk celery
- 2 cloves garlic
- 1 ½ teaspoons unrefined salt
- 1 cup water

Servings: 4
Prep time: 5-10 minutes

LIMA BEANS

Directions:

1. Blend the onion, celery, and garlic with 1 cup of water and place with beans in a 2-quart sauce pan.
2. Fill the sauce pan with enough water so that there is 1 inch of water above the level of the beans.
3. Bring beans to a boil, then cover and simmer the beans at lower heat for approximately 1 hour. Add salt and cook for 5 more minutes or until soft.

Ingredients:

- ½ cup parsley, finely chopped
- ½ onion, finely chopped
- 2 roma tomatoes, diced
- ¼ cup olives, finely chopped (optional)
- ½ cup red or yellow bell pepper, diced
- 2 teaspoons lemon juice (fresh lemon)
- ¼ teaspoon unrefined salt, or to taste

Servings: 4
Prep time: 20 minutes for toppings
Cook Time: 1 hour for beans

LIMA BEAN TOPPINGS

Directions:

1. Prepare the raw toppings individually and mix, or cut coarsely and place all ingredients into a food processor and process, pulsing until a chunky pico de gallo consistency.

Ingredients:

- 1-pound yuca root (the equivalent of approximately 1-foot by 2-inch diameter of fresh yuca root)
- ½ teaspoon unrefined salt, or to taste
- ¼ teaspoon garlic powder, or to taste
- ½ cup coconut milk (see index)

Servings: 4
Prep time for yuca: 15 minutes
Prep time for milk: 15 minutes
Cook time: 45 minutes

COOKED YUCA

Yuca is a high fiber starchy plant. It can be found in the produce section or pre-peeled and cored in the freezer section. Tapioca is a product made from yuca.

Directions:

1. Cut yuca root into 2-inch lengths and remove the brown waxy outer skin carefully with knife. Split each piece in half and remove fibrous core.
2. Place in medium saucepan, cover with two inches water and add salt.
3. Cover saucepan and cook on low heat for about 45 minutes or until tender.
4. Blend the coconut milk with garlic powder and salt.
5. Pour the blended milk over the yuca before serving.

Ingredients:

- 2 cups of broccoli, cut into florets.
- 1 cup water
- 1 tablespoon of lemon
- Unrefined salt to taste
- Optional: Super Antioxidant Seasoning (see index)
- Optional: garlic powder, to taste

Servings: 4
Prep time: 5 minutes
Cook Time: 7 minutes

STEAMED BROCCOLI

Directions:

1. Place a steamer basket into a medium saucepan and fill with about an inch of water. Bring to a boil.
2. Add broccoli florets, cover, lower heat, and steam for 5-7 minutes.
3. Remove the broccoli florets and place into a serving bowl. Season with lemon juice, salt and garlic powder to taste.

Serve with Mixed Green Salad. Please see page 103 for recipe.

BREAKFAST **DAY 2**

*Cooked Amaranth Cereal, Sunflower Power Smoothie,
Flatbread, and Seed Butter*

*Flatbread and seed butter can be prepared days to weeks in advance.
Both freeze well so that you can take your time to consume them!*

Ingredients:

- 1 cup amaranth, soaked overnight and rinsed
- 2 cups water
- ½ teaspoon unrefined salt
- ½ cup milk of choice
- ½ teaspoon of honey
- 1 ½ cups berries
- ¼ teaspoon of cardamom (optional)
- ¼ teaspoon of coriander (optional)

Servings: 4
Prep time: 5 minutes
Cook time: 30 minutes

COOKED AMARANTH CEREAL

Amaranth cereal (and all the cooked cereals) can be cooked and then stored in the refrigerator for up to 3-4 days.

Directions:

1. In a saucepan, bring amaranth, salt and water to a boil.
2. Cover and simmer on low for 30 minutes, until all the water is fully absorbed. Stir often.
3. Serve with a plant-based milk and sweeten with honey.
4. Garnish with fresh berries, coriander and cardamom.

Ingredients:

- 2 tablespoons sunflower seeds, soaked
- 1 tablespoon chia seeds
- ½ cup berries
- 1 Granny Smith apple
- 2 tablespoons shredded coconut
- 2 tablespoons carob powder
- ¾ cup water

Servings: 12 ounces, one serving
Prep time: 5-10 minutes

SUNFLOWER POWER SMOOTHIE

Directions:

1. Blend all ingredients and serve

Serve with flatbread and seed butter of choice (see p. 89-91).

LUNCH **DAY 2**

Garden Potato Meal: Potatoes with Guacamole and Salsa, Pinto Beans, and Red Cabbage Salad

Beans are a convenient food for meal prepping. They can be prepared in advance and frozen in meal-sized containers for convenience. Remember to start soaking them at least 12-24 hours in advance of cooking.

GARDEN POTATO
MEAL POTATOES

Ingredients:

- 4 large russet potatoes

Servings: 4
Prep time: 5 minutes
Cook time: 30 minutes

Directions:

1. Place a steamer basket into a medium saucepan. Fill with water to just below steamer basket. Place washed and unpeeled potatoes into the steamer basket and cover. Bring water to a boil, then lower heat to simmer. Steam potatoes for approximately 30 minutes. Potatoes are done when pierced easily with a fork or a knife.
2. Cut steamed potatoes in half, lengthwise.

SIDE OF PINTO BEANS

Ingredients:

- 2 cups beans, soaked overnight and rinsed
- ½ onion
- 1 stalk celery
- 2 cloves garlic
- 1 ½ teaspoon unrefined salt
- 1 cup water

Servings: 4 servings
Prep time: 5-10 minutes
Cook time: 1 hour

Directions:

1. Place beans in a 2-quart saucepan and fill with water to one inch above the level of the beans.
2. Blend onion, celery, and garlic with 1 cup of water and add to the saucepan.
3. Cook until beans are soft, approximately 1 hour.
4. Add salt and cook for 5 more minutes.

Serve with the red cabbage salad. Please see page 103 for recipe.

Toppings

SALSA

Ingredients:

- ¼ cup onion, finely chopped
- 3 tomatoes (medium), diced
- ¼ cup red or yellow bell pepper, diced
- 2 teaspoons lemon juice (fresh lemon)
- ½ cup cilantro, chopped
- ½ teaspoon unrefined salt, or to taste

Servings: 4 cups of salsa
Prep time: 10 minutes using food processor

Directions:

1. Prepare the raw toppings individually and mix.
2. If using a food processor, cut coarsely, place all ingredients (except tomatoes) into a food processor and pulse until lightly processed.
3. Add coarsely chopped tomatoes last into processor and pulse until adequately processed. Processing the tomatoes last keeps the salsa chunky, without being "soupy".
4. Allow the mixture to sit for about 30 minutes before serving.

GUACAMOLE

Ingredients:

- 2 avocados
- 2 teaspoons lemon juice
- ¼ teaspoon unrefined salt

Servings: 1 cup guacamole
Prep time: 5 minutes

Directions:

1. In a medium-sized mixing bowl, mash avocados. Mix in lemon juice and salt.

BREAKFAST **DAY 3**

Sweet Potatoes, Coconut Cheese, Pumpkin Power Smoothie, Flatbread, Seed butter

Sweet potatoes are a rich source of Vitamins A and B. They also provide many minerals, protein, and fiber. Another sweet thing is that they take very little time or effort to prepare.

SWEET POTATOES

Ingredients:

- 4 sweet potatoes, preferably Asian sweet potatoes

Servings: 4
Prep time: 5 minutes
Cook Time: 45 minutes to 1 hour

Directions for baking:

1. Line baking tray with unbleached parchment paper. Place the thoroughly washed and unpeeled sweet potatoes onto the parchment paper.
2. Bake at 400 degrees for one hour. Check if sweet potatoes are ready by piercing them with a butter knife. They should be tender through and through.

Directions for steaming:

1. Place a steamer basket into a medium-sized sauce pan.
2. Fill the saucepan with water to just below the steamer basket.
3. Place washed and unpeeled sweet potatoes into the steamer basket.
4. Bring water to a boil, then cover and simmer until the sweet potatoes are thoroughly tender when pierced with a butter knife. (Approximately 40 minutes).

Serve slices of sweet potatoes topped with coconut cheese

Ingredients:

- 2½ cups coconut milk
- 2 teaspoons unrefined salt
- 2 tablespoons agar powder (not flakes)
- 3 tablespoons arrowroot powder
- 2 teaspoons lemon juice
- ¼ cup sunflower seed, soaked overnight and rinsed (optional)
- ½ teaspoon Super Antioxidant Seasoning (optional), (see index)

Prep time: 10 minutes
Cook Time: 10-15 minutes

COCONUT CHEESE

Directions:

1. Blend all ingredients until smooth.
2. Pour the blend into a saucepan and bring to a boil, stirring constantly.
3. When the blend comes to a boil, lower heat and simmer until thick. Stir constantly.
4. Remove from heat.
5. If you plan to serve right away, pour the mixture into a glass container and place into the freezer for a half hour to set. Otherwise, place the glass container into the fridge to harden and to store.

Leftovers: Store covered in the refrigerator up to five days. May use also as a spread for bread.

Ingredients:

- 2 tablespoons pumpkin seeds, soaked
- 1 tablespoon flaxseed
- ½ cup berries
- 1 apple
- 2 tablespoons shredded coconut
- 2 tablespoons carob powder
- ¾ cup water

Servings: 12 ounces, one serving
Prep time: 5-10 minutes

PUMPKIN SEED PROTEIN SMOOTHIE

Directions:

1. Blend all ingredients and serve.

Serve with flatbread and seed butter of choice (see p. 89-91).

LUNCH **DAY 3**

Quinoa Rice, Kidney Beans, Ceviche, with Red Cabbage Salad

These dishes are bursting with color—that means lots of antioxidants— and flavor!

Ingredients:

- 1 cup quinoa, soaked 8 hours and rinsed
- 1 cup water
- 1 garlic clove, minced
- ¼ cup chopped onion
- ½ teaspoon unrefined salt

Servings: 4
Prep time: 10 minutes
Cook Time: 20 minutes

QUINOA RICE

Directions:

1. Place all ingredients into a medium-sized saucepan.
2. Bring contents to a boil, then cover and decrease heat to simmer.
3. Cook for about 15-20 minutes until all the liquid has been absorbed and quinoa is tender and fluffy.

Ingredients:

- 2 cups beans soaked 24 hours and rinse twice a day
- 1/2 onion
- 1 stalk celery
- 2 cloves garlic
- 2 teaspoons unrefined salt
- 1 cup water for blending

Servings: 4
Prep time: 10 minutes
Cook Time: 1 hour

KIDNEY BEANS

Directions:

1. Place beans into a 2-quart saucepan and fill with water to one inch above the level of the beans.
2. Blend onion, celery, and garlic with 1 cup of water and add to the beans.
3. Bring to a boil and then simmer until the beans are soft (approximately 1 hour)
4. Add the salt and cook for 5 more minutes.

Ingredients:

- 2 cups cauliflower, pulsed in a food processor until finely processed
- 1 cucumber, finely chopped
- 1 Roma tomato, diced
- ½ cups cilantro, chopped (may use parsley)
- ⅓ cup red onion, finely chopped
- ¼ cup lime juice
- Unrefined salt to taste
- Cayenne pepper to taste

Servings: 4
Prep time: 20 minutes

CEVICHE

Directions:

1. Coarsely chop cauliflower and process finely. Place processed cauliflower into a medium sized mixing bowl.
2. Chop the cilantro into very small pieces (approximately 1/2 inch) and place into food processor. Cilantro will not process very well unless chopped finely beforehand.
3. Cut the remaining vegetables coarsely and place all into a food processor and process.
4. Place the mixture into a mixing bowl with cauliflower and mix with lime juice.
5. Sprinkle with unrefined salt and cayenne pepper to taste.
6. To serve, plate out quinoa, beans, ceviche, and red cabbage salad (p. 103).

BREAKFAST **DAY 4**

*Chia Seed Pudding, Pumpkin Seed Protein Power Smoothie,
Flatbread, and Seed Butter*

*This is an easy, tasty dish for breakfast. There is a whole lot
of nutrition packed into these tiny seeds!*

Ingredients:

- ½ cup chia seed
- 2 cups coconut milk
- ½ teaspoon vanilla
- 1 tablespoon honey and 1 teaspoon stevia leaf powder
- ½ cup berries

Servings: 4
Prep time: 10 minutes

CHIA SEED PUDDING

Directions:

1. Blend milk, vanilla, honey and stevia.
2. Pour into a 1 liter jar and add chia seeds.
3. Allow to sit for 5-10 minutes, then stir.
4. Refrigerate overnight before serving.
5. Garnish with berries.

Ingredients:

- 2 tablespoons sunflower seeds, soaked
- 1 tablespoon chia seeds
- ½ cup berries
- 1 Granny Smith apple
- 2 tablespoons shredded coconut
- 2 tablespoons carob powder
- ¾ cup water

Servings: 12 ounces, one serving
Prep time: 5-10 minutes

SUNFLOWER POWER SMOOTHIE

Directions:

1. Blend all ingredients and serve.

Serve with flatbread and seed butter of choice (see p. 89-91).

LUNCH **DAY 4**

Red Lentils, Potato Salad, Broccoli, and Green Salad

This lunch provides a garden of color to the eyes and of taste to the palate!

Ingredients:

- 2 cups red lentils soaked for 8 hours and rinsed
- 1 carrot, diced
- 1 tablespoon onion powder
- 1 teaspoon garlic powder
- 1 ½ teaspoons unrefined salt

Servings: 4
Prep time: 5-10 minutes
Cook time: 20 minutes

Ingredients:

- 4 red potatoes
- ½ cup broccoli florets
- ½ cup cauliflower florets
- ½ zucchini cut into small cubes
- ¼ red onion, finely chopped
- ¼ red or orange bell pepper, finely chopped
- ¼ cup green onion, finely chopped
- 1 teaspoon of Super Antioxidant Seasoning (see index)
- 1 tablespoon of freshly squeezed lemon juice
- Unrefined salt to taste

Servings: 4
Prep time: 15 minutes
Cook time: 20 minutes

RED LENTILS

Directions:

1. Place soaked lentils, carrot, onion powder, and garlic powder into a 2-quart sauce pan and fill with water to one inch above the level of the lentils.
2. Bring water to boil, then reduce heat and simmer.
3. When lentils are soft (approximately 15 minutes), add the salt and cook for 5 more minutes.

POTATO SALAD

Directions:

1. Place a steamer basket into a medium saucepan. Fill with one-two inches of water, or to just below the steamer basket.
2. Place potatoes into steamer basket. Cover saucepan and bring to a boil. Lower the heat and steam potatoes for 15-20 minutes. Potatoes should be tender through and through when done.
3. Place a steamer basket into a small saucepan. Fill with one inch of water and place broccoli, cauliflower, and zucchini into the steamer basket. Steam vegetables for approximately 5-7 minutes (don't overcook).
4. Drain and place vegetables into a serving bowl.
5. When potatoes are cool, cut into cubes and add to cooked vegetables.
6. Add red onion, bell pepper, green onion, seasoning, lemon juice, and salt. Mix well.

Serve with Mixed Green Salad. Please see page 103 for recipe.

BREAKFAST **DAY 5**

*Cooked Buckwheat Cereal, Pumpkin Seed Protein
Power Smoothie, Flatbread, and Seed Butter*

*This is a convenient way to use buckwheat.
Make sure you use plenty of berries with your cereal and smoothie!*

Ingredients:

- 1 cup hulled raw buckwheat groats, soaked overnight and rinsed
- 2 cups water
- ½ teaspoon unrefined salt
- ½ teaspoon of honey
- 1 ½ cups berries
- ¼ teaspoon of cardamom
- ¼ teaspoon of coriander
- 2 cups plant-based milk of your choosing (see index)

Servings: 3-4
Prep time: 5 minutes
Cook time: 20 minutes

COOKED BUCKWHEAT CEREAL

Directions:

1. In a covered saucepan bring buckwheat, salt and water to rolling boil.
2. Lower heat and simmer for 15-20 minutes until the water is fully absorbed.
3. Serve with milk and sweeten with ½ teaspoon honey.
4. Garnish with fresh berries, coriander and cardamom.

Ingredients:

- 2 tablespoons pumpkin seeds, soaked
- 1 tablespoon flaxseed
- ½ cup berries
- 1 apple
- 2 tablespoons shredded coconut
- 2 tablespoons carob powder
- ¾ cup water

Servings: 12 ounces, one serving
Prep time: 5-10 minutes

PUMPKIN SEED PROTEIN SMOOTHIE

Directions:

1. Blend all ingredients and serve.

Serve with flatbread and seed butter of choice (see p. 89-91).

LUNCH **DAY 5**

Cauliflower Rice, Pinto Beans, Salad, Flatbread

This cauliflower rice recipe provides lots of raw vegetables, brimming with digestive enzymes, probiotics, and prebiotics--especially if you grow your own produce!

Ingredients:

- ½ head cauliflower coarsely chopped
- 1 tomato, chopped into large chunks
- 1 bell pepper, chopped, large pieces
- ½ cup cilantro, chopped
- 1 green onion, thinly sliced
- ⅛ teaspoon cayenne pepper
- 2 tablespoons lemon juice
- 1 avocado, mashed
- 1 ½ teaspoons paprika
- 1 teaspoon unrefined salt
- ½ teaspoon homemade chili powder (p, 107)

Servings: 4
Prep time: 20 minutes
Cook time: 30 minutes

CAULIFLOWER RICE

Directions:

1. Pulse cauliflower in the food processor until they resemble small grains of rice.
2. Place processed cauliflower in a serving bowl.
3. Add the bell pepper and chopped cilantro to the food processor and pulse. The cilantro should be chopped into half-inch pieces prior to placing into processor.
4. Add tomatoes to the processor and pulse the mixture further. Processing the tomatoes last prevents the processed mixture from becoming too "soupy".
5. Add the processed mixture to the serving bowl.
6. Chop the green onion finely and add to the bowl.
7. Gently mix all ingredients together.
8. Chill approximately 30 minutes before serving.

PINTO BEANS

Directions:

1. Place beans into a 2-quart sauce pan.
2. Fill with water to one inch above the level the beans.
3. Add the remaining ingredients, except for the salt.
4. Bring water to a boil, then lower heat and simmer until the beans are soft, approximately 1 hour.
5. Add the salt and cook for 5 more minutes.

Serve with a green salad (p. 103), crackers (pp. 95-96), or gluten free bread (p.89)

Ingredients:

- 2 cups beans soaked overnight and rinsed
- 1 tablespoon onion powder
- 2 teaspoons garlic powder
- 1 teaspoon cumin
- 1 teaspoon oregano
- 1 tomato, chopped
- 2 teaspoons unrefined salt

Servings: 4
Prep time: 5-10 minutes
Cook time: 1 hour

BREAKFAST **DAY 6**

*Non-Fried French Fries, Breakfast Patties,
Sun Power Smoothies, Flatbread, Seed Butter*

*There are a lot of cooked foods in this meal, so don't skip your smoothie
and seed butters.*

NON-FRIED FRENCH FRIES

Ingredients:

- 3 large Russet potatoes
- 1 teaspoon unrefined salt, or to taste
- 1 teaspoon garlic powder
- 1 tablespoon onion powder
- 2 tablespoons ground flaxseed
- 1 tablespoon dill seasoning

Servings: 4
Prep time: 5-10 minutes
Cook time: 40 minutes

Directions:

1. Cut potatoes into long strips so they look like thick French fries.
2. Place steamer basket into a medium-sized sauce pan and fill with water until the water is just below the steamer basket.
3. Place cut potatoes into the steamer basket and cover.
4. Bring water to a boil and then lower heat to simmer for about 10 minutes.
5. When tender but still firm, drain the residual water and place potatoes into a large bowl. (You don't want the potatoes to be too soft).
6. Mix all the remaining ingredients together in another small bowl.
7. Sprinkle the mixed seasoning mixture over the potatoes and mix well.
8. Arrange potatoes on a baking sheet lined with parchment paper.
9. Bake for 25 minutes at 375 degrees until crispy.

Ingredients:

- ½ cup mung beans, soaked overnight and rinsed
- 1 tablespoon onion powder
- 1 teaspoon garlic powder
- ½ cup pumpkin seed, soaked overnight and rinsed
- ½ cup chopped onions
- 2 small cloves garlic, minced
- 1 medium potato, cooked
- 2 tablespoons ground flaxseed
- ½ teaspoon salt

Prep time: 15-20 minutes
Cook time: 30 minutes
Bake time: 30 minutes

MUNG BEAN BREAKFAST PATTY

Directions:

1. Place mung beans, onion powder, and garlic powder into a small saucepan and cover with one inch of water.
2. Bring water to a boil, then lower heat and simmer for approximately 35 min, or until soft, but not overdone.
3. Add salt and cook 5 minutes more.
4. Drain the mung beans and place them into a mixing bowl.
5. Process pumpkin seeds finely and add to the mixing bowl.
6. Add potato to the processor and process finely. Place in the mixing bowl.
7. Add chopped onion, minced garlic, ground flaxseeds and salt to the mixing bowl.
8. Mix all the ingredients well.
9. Line a baking tray with parchment paper.
10. Use the lid of a small-mouthed canning jar to form the patties and place the patties on the lined tray.
11. Bake at 375 degrees for 20 minutes, turn the patties, and bake an additional 10 minutes, or until browned.

Ingredients:

- 2 tablespoons sunflower seeds, soaked
- 1 tablespoon chia seed
- ½ cup berries
- 1 Granny Smith apple
- 2 tablespoons shredded coconut
- 2 tablespoons carob powder
- ¾ cup water

Servings: 12 ounces, one serving
Prep time: 5-10 minutes

Directions:

1. Blend all ingredients.

Serve with flatbread and seed butter of choice (see p. 89-91).

71

LUNCH **DAY 6**

*Asian Sweet Potatoes with Raw Pesto Sauce,
Garbanzo Beans, Steamed Broccoli, Green Salad*

The pesto sauce is a very convenient way to include greens into your diet.

Ingredients:

- 4 Asian sweet potatoes

Ingredients:

- 1 avocado
- 2 green onions
- Juice of 1 lemon
- ½ red bell pepper
- 2 cloves garlic
- ¼ teaspoon unrefined salt, or to taste
- 2 tablespoons sunflower seeds, soaked overnight, optional

Add any of the following combinations of greens:

- 1 cup spinach and 1 cup cilantro
- ½ cup basil and 1 cup parsley
- 1 cup cilantro and 1 cup parsley

Servings: 4
Prep time: 15 minutes
Cook time: 45 minutes

ASIAN SWEET POTATOES

Directions:

1. Steam sweet potatoes until tender when pierced through with a fork (about 40 minutes). Refer to page 53 for more detailed instructions.
2. Drain water immediately and cut in half, lengthwise.
3. Top with the pesto sauce.

NUTRITIONAL PESTO SAUCE

Directions:

1. Blend all ingredients until smooth. Serve.

Ingredients:

- 2 cups garbanzo beans soaked overnight, rinsed
- 1 onion, cut in half
- ½ stalk celery, cut in half
- 1-2 teaspoons unrefined salt, to taste

Servings: 4
Prep time: 5 minutes
Cook time: 1 hour

GARBANZO BEANS

Directions:

1. Place beans into a 2-quart sauce pot and fill with water to one inch above the level of the beans.
2. Add onion halves and celery.
3. Bring to a boil and then lower heat and simmer until beans are soft, approximately 1 hour. Add salt and cook for 5 more minutes.
4. Remove onion and celery prior to serving.

Ingredients:

- 2 cups of broccoli, cut into florets.
- 1 cup water
- 1 tablespoon of lemon
- Salt to taste
- Optional: garlic powder

Servings: 4
Prep time: 5 minutes
Cook time: 7 minutes

STEAMED BROCCOLI

Directions:

1. Place a steamer basket into a medium saucepan and fill with about an inch of water. Bring to a boil.
2. Add broccoli florets, cover, lower heat, and steam for 5-7 minutes.
3. Remove the broccoli florets and place into a serving bowl. Season with lemon juice, salt and garlic powder to taste.

Serve with Mixed Green Salad. Please see page 103 for recipe.

BREAKFAST **DAY 7**

Quinoa Breakfast Cereal, Pumpkin Seed Protein Smoothie, Flatbread, Seed Butter

Quinoa is a good source of protein and fiber. It's also loaded with minerals. Here is a delightfully delicious way to have quinoa!

Ingredients:

- 1 cup quinoa, soaked overnight and rinsed
- 2 cups water
- ¼ teaspoon unrefined salt
- ½-1 teaspoon honey
- 1½ cups berries
- ¼ teaspoon of cardamom (optional)
- ¼ teaspoon of coriander (optional)
- 2 cups plant-based milk of your choosing

Servings: 4
Prep time: 5 minutes
Cook time: 20 minutes

QUINOA BREAKFAST CEREAL

Directions:

1. In a saucepan, bring quinoa, salt and water to a rolling boil.
2. Cover, lower heat, and simmer for 15-20 minutes until water is fully absorbed, stirring occasionally.
3. Serve with milk and sweeten with honey.
4. Garnish with fresh berries, coriander, and cardamom.

Ingredients:

- 2 tablespoons pumpkin seeds, soaked overnight
- 1 tablespoon flaxseed
- ½ cup berries
- 1 apple
- 2 tablespoons shredded coconut
- 2 tablespoons carob powder
- ¾ cup water

Servings: 12 ounces, one serving
Prep time: 5-10 minutes

PUMPKIN SEED PROTEIN SMOOTHIE

Directions:

1. Blend all ingredients and serve

Serve with flatbread and seed butter of choice (see index).

LUNCH **DAY 7**

*Potato Layer Fiesta with Cream, Guacamole and Salsa,
Lentils, Steamed Kale, and Green Salad*

*This is the meal that Mercy serves to clients when they arrive at the Years
Restored program. It works best with a springform mold pan, as this allows
you to remove the pan with the least disturbance to the dish.
But use whichever pan you have!*

Potato Layer Fiesta

Prepare each layer of the ingredients as directed and assemble as per directions below. This is served with a side dish of lentils and salad.

Ingredients:

- 5 red or yellow potatoes, unpeeled
- 1 teaspoon onion powder
- 2 teaspoons unrefined salt, or to taste
- ½ teaspoon garlic powder
- ½ cup coconut milk

Servings: 4
Prep time: 5 minutes
Cook Time: 45 minutes to 1 hour

MASHED POTATOES

Directions:

1. Place a steamer basket into a medium saucepan. Fill with water to just under the steamer basket.
2. Place potatoes into the steamer basket and cover.
3. Bring water to a boil, then lower heat and simmer potatoes until tender when pierced through with a fork, (about 25 minutes). Time varies depending upon size of the potatoes.
4. Drain water and place potatoes into a large mixing bowl.
5. Mix in onion and garlic powder, coconut milk and salt.
6. Mash until creamy.

Ingredients:

- 2 cups sunflower seeds, soaked overnight and rinsed
- 1 small clove garlic
- 1 tablespoon fresh red onion
- ½ red bell pepper (seeds removed)
- 1 cup water
- 1 tablespoon lemon juice
- ½-1 teaspoon unrefined salt, or to taste

VEGGIE CREAM

Directions:

1. Blend until smooth.

GUACAMOLE

Ingredients:

- 3 avocados
- 1 tablespoon lemon juice
- ½ - 1 teaspoon unrefined salt, or to taste

Directions:

1. Mix avocado with lemon juice and salt and mash and mix well.

Ingredients:

- ¼ red or yellow onion coarsely chopped
- ¼ red or yellow bell pepper, coarsely chopped
- Juice of 1 lemon
- ½ cup cilantro, chopped (may use parsley)
- 3 tomatoes (medium), coarsely chopped
- ½ teaspoon unrefined salt, or to taste

Servings: 4-5
Prep time: 45 minutes
Cook time: 30 minutes

SALSA

Directions:

1. Add onion, bell pepper, lemon juice, cilantro and salt to a food processor.
2. Pulse all ingredients briefly to a chunky consistency.
3. Add tomatoes and pulse again. Adding tomatoes last helps keeps the salsa from being too "soupy".

ASSEMBLING THE POTATO FIESTA

Directions:

1. To assemble the layers, place mashed potato into a springform mold or a casserole dish and press down firmly with serving utensil.
2. Add a layer of veggie cream, then a layer of guacamole, and top with salsa.
3. Cut into portion-sized pieces and serve using a spatula.

Ingredients:

- 2 cups brown lentils, soaked and rinsed
- 1 tablespoon onion powder
- 1 teaspoon garlic powder
- 1 ½ teaspoons unrefined salt, or to taste

Servings: 4
Prep time: 5-10 minutes
Cook time: 30-45 minutes

BROWN LENTILS

Directions:

1. Place lentils, onion powder, and garlic powder in a 2-quart saucepan and fill with water to 1 inch above the level of the lentils.
2. Cook until lentils are soft (approximately 30 minutes).
3. Add salt and cook for 5 more minutes.

Ingredients:

- 1 bunch of kale, trimmed of stems and chopped
- 2 cloves of garlic, minced
- 1 tablespoon of fresh lemon juice
- Sprinkled unrefined salt to taste

Servings: 4
Prep time: 10 minutes
Cook time: 5 minutes

STEAMED KALE

Directions:

1. Place chopped kale and minced garlic into a steamer basket and steam kale until wilted, approximately 5 minutes.
2. Sprinkle with lemon juice and salt, and mix well.

Serve with Mixed Green Salad. Please see page 103 for recipe.

PART IV

ADDITIONAL RECIPES:
BREAKFAST

BASIC BUCKWHEAT

We love the delightful crunchiness of this cereal. Process larger quantities of buckwheat that can be dehydrated and stored in the freezer in airtight containers. You can use as a breakfast cereal, or as a topping for parfaits and sweet potatoes.

Ingredients:

- 3 cups raw, hulled, buckwheat groats
- 64 oz Mason jar or medium sized glass bowl

Directions:

1. Place Buckwheat groats in Mason jar and rinse. Soak for 30 minutes to 8 hours. Rinse off the viscous fluid that develops.
2. Sprout for 2 days, rinsing at least twice a day. Don't over sprout, or it will develop an odor.
3. When sprouts are at least as long as the body of the groats, dehydrate at 109 degrees F for 18 hours.
4. Store in airtight containers and use as you would dry cereal.

RAW BERRY GRANOLA

Three cups of raw buckwheat will sprout into about 9 cups of buckwheat! You will use it all to make the granola.

Ingredients:

- 3 cups raw buckwheat groats, sprouted for 2 days, rinsing at least twice a day. (See Basic Buckwheat recipe or Sprouting Section)
- ½ cup sunflower seeds, soaked overnight and rinsed
- ½ cup pumpkin seeds, soaked overnight and rinsed
- 1½ cups shredded coconut (fresh or dried)
- 1 banana
- ⅓ cup raw honey
- 1 tablespoon alcohol-free vanilla or 1-inch piece of vanilla bean
- 2 cups blueberries, strawberries, blackberries or a combination of all
- 1 teaspoon stevia (ground whole leaf powder)
- 1 teaspoon unrefined salt

Directions:

1. Place sprouted buckwheat groats, sunflower seeds, pumpkin seeds, and shredded coconut into a bowl.
2. Place banana, honey, vanilla, berries, stevia, and salt into high speed blender until creamy.
3. Pour over the ingredients in the bowl and mix well until all ingredients are covered.
4. Arrange on dehydrator trays lined with parchment paper.
5. Dehydrate at 109 degrees for 24 hours total or until dry and crunchy.
6. Store in the refrigerator for long term storage.

Peruvian Breakfast Pancake

This is a good recipe to make if you have leftover cooked quinoa. Use 2 cups of cooked quinoa if you're using leftover cooked quinoa. We bake these in the oven, rather than using the range.

Ingredients:

- 1 cup of quinoa, soaked overnight and rinsed
- ½ cup sunflower seeds, soaked overnight
- ¼ cup tapioca or arrowroot flour
- 2 teaspoons vanilla
- 1 tablespoon honey
- ¼ teaspoon salt
- 1½ cups water

Directions:

1. Place quinoa into saucepan with 1 cup of water.
2. Bring water to a boil and then simmer covered for 15 minutes or until water is absorbed.
3. Place cooked quinoa and all other ingredients into a high-speed blender and blend all ingredients until smooth. Add more water if needed to attain a pancake batter consistency.
4. Line baking sheets with parchment paper.
5. Pour a half-cup of the batter onto the baking sheets and use a spatula to spread each pancake into circles that are approximately six inches in diameter.
6. Bake in a preheated 400-degree oven for 15-20 minutes, then turn over and continue baking for 5-10 minutes more.
7. Serve as you would regular pancakes.

Servings: 12 pancakes.

Berry Jam

Ingredients:

- 2 cups frozen or fresh berries
- 1 teaspoon honey
- ½ teaspoon stevia leaf

Directions:

1. Blend all ingredients together and use as topping for bread or waffle.

- -

Milk and Whipped Cream

Many of these will be used for breakfast foods. Some, like seed butters, can be used for either breakfast or lunch.

Pumpkin Carob Milk

This is a very simple recipe that gives a tasty milk. Strain through a fine mesh strainer if you wish. Blackstrap molasses may take some getting used to if you haven't tried it before, but it is a sweetener that is also a great source of minerals and vitamins.

Ingredients:

- 4 cups of water
- 1 cup of soaked pumpkin seeds
- 4 tablespoons of roasted carob
- 1 tablespoon of honey or blackstrap molasses
- 1 teaspoon stevia herb
- 2 teaspoons vanilla extract
- 1 pinch of unrefined salt

Directions:

1. Blend all ingredients on high. Serve.

SUNFLOWER SEED MILK

A very nice flavored milk that can be made quickly!

Ingredients:

- 1 cup sunflower seeds, soaked and rinsed
- 3 cups water
- 1 tablespoon honey
- 1 teaspoon Stevia herb (ground whole leaf powder)
- 1 green apple
- 1 tablespoon vanilla (alcohol free)

Directions:

1. Blend well at high speed.
2. Strain with a nut milk bag or fine mesh strainer if desired.

QUICK COCONUT MILK

There is nothing like coconut milk from a fresh coconut; but on the days when you are running late, this is a great substitute.

Ingredients:

- 1 cup dehydrated coconut flakes
- 1½ cups hot water

Directions:

1. Blend well at high speed.
2. Let it set for about 20 minutes.
3. Strain with a nut milk bag or fine mesh strainer if desired.

* * * * * * * * * * * * * * * * * * * *

Coconuts

You will notice that none of our recipes call for canned or boxed coconut milk or water; the most processed ingredient in our recipes is the dehydrated coconut flakes. We have found that the incredible flavor and consistency of the fresh coconut makes it worth the effort. If you aren't used to using coconuts, we recommend starting with the young coconuts, which are easier to open, have a softer meat that is easier to remove, and have a milder sweeter flavor. In our coconut milk recipes, we have included detailed instruction for opening the young and mature coconuts. Check autoimmuneplantbased.com or drjoycechoe.com for instructional videos.

YOUNG COCONUT MILK

Coconut milk fresh from the coconut takes more time, but nothing beats the flavor!

Ingredients:

- Meat of 1 young coconut, approximately 1 cup
- Fine mesh strainer

Directions:

1. Wash the coconut well.
2. Using a large knife and with the coconut placed on a firm surface, begin chopping firmly all the way around the top of the coconut. Make the opening as wide as you can. Continue chopping all the way around. You want to enter into the coconut when you have evenly made your chops 360 degrees around the top of the coconut, rather than staying in any one position, because the coconut water will start to spill out after the shell is penetrated.
3. When you have entered into the coconut, use the tip of the knife to deepen the hole and try to open the coconut without spilling the water. Place the strainer over the blender container and pour coconut water into the container through the strainer.
4. Shell the meat out of the coconut by using the back of a spoon or a coconut tool, depending how mature and firm the coconut is and how much meat is inside. If the meat is not well developed, you may need the meat of another young coconut to make enough milk.
5. Place the meat into a high-speed blender. Remove coconut water or add pure water so that the water just covers the coconut meat. Blend thoroughly and serve.

MATURE COCONUT MILK

Mature coconuts have much more meat and provide much more milk than young coconuts. They provide a nice rich flavor that is not as sweet as younger coconuts. Mature coconuts require a little bit more physical exertion to crack open and to extract meat, but the milk is well worth the effort!

Ingredients:

- 1 mature coconut
- Strong plastic bag (i.e. bags for potatoes)
- Reusable nut milk bag

Directions:

1. Wash the coconut well. At the bottom of the coconut are three circles. Puncture the softest of the three circles with a knife and drain the coconut water into a bowl.
2. Place the coconut in a strong plastic bag and strike it on the ground outside or use a hammer to crack it.
3. Use a coconut tool or a butter knife to separate the meat from the shell.
4. Rinse well to remove all pieces of shell.
5. Place the meat into a blender. Fill the blender container with water, so that the water line is at the same level as the coconut pieces. Use plain water and not the coconut water, which in mature coconuts tends to have too strong a flavor. Blend well.
6. Place the blended milk into the nut milk bag and use both hands to squeeze out milk.
7. Store the milk in the refrigerator for up to three days.

COCONUT WHIPPED CREAM

A variation of coconut cream that can be used with parfaits, waffles, pancakes, and sweet potatoes.

Ingredients:

- ½ cup sunflower seeds, soaked and rinsed
- The meat of 1 young coconut

- ½ cup coconut water
- 1 tablespoon lemon juice
- 1 tablespoon honey
- 1 teaspoon Stevia herb (ground whole leaf powder)
- 1 teaspoon vanilla
- Pinch salt

Directions:

1. Blend the above on high speed until creamy and chill in the freezer for about 20 minutes before serving.

• • • • • • • • • • • • • • • • • • • •

Breads

We do not include any breads with yeast, as many people with leaky gut are sensitive to them. The medium used to grow yeast can be derived from wheat and other grains. The media can also be genetically modified. We use flatbreads, tortillas, wraps, crackers, pancakes, and waffles to satiate the desire for bread.

POTATO FLATBREAD

This recipe produces an easy bread that has a wonderful flavor. Cut in half and use for sandwiches or breakfast breads with coconut cheese or seed butter.

Ingredients:

- 1 cup sprouted quinoa or buckwheat flour
- ½ cup flax seed, ground
- 2 medium potatoes, steamed

- 1 teaspoon unrefined salt
- Optional: ¼ teaspoon of the following: sage, onion powder, marjoram and rosemary

Directions:

1. Place a steamer basket into a medium saucepan and fill with enough water to bring water level to just below the steamer basket.
2. Place potatoes into the steamer basket and cover. Bring water to a boil and then lower heat so that the water is gently boiling to steam the potatoes for 15-20 minutes.
3. Mash potatoes, and mix in the other ingredients until the mixture achieves the consistency of bread dough (you may use a food processor).
4. Place 1 large spoonful onto your hand and roll into a ball. If the dough is too moist and too sticky to work with, sprinkle quinoa flour into the dough until it is not sticky.

5. Place onto a baking tray lined with parchment paper and flatten into a flatbread shape (round like a biscuit) that is a half-inch thick and about three inches in diameter.
6. Bake at 400 degrees F for about 25 minutes, until lightly golden.

PLANTAIN FLATBREAD

Plantain provides a wonderful sweet flavor to the bread.

Ingredients:

- 1 ripe large plantain (approximately about 1 lb.)
- 1 cup sprouted quinoa flour
- ½ cup flax seed, ground
- ½ teaspoon unrefined salt
- 2 teaspoons vanilla

Directions:

1. Peel and mash plantain in a food processor.
2. Mix in the other ingredients until the mixture resembles the consistency of bread dough.
3. Place 1 large spoonful onto your hand and form it into a ball. If the dough is too moist and too sticky to work with, sprinkle quinoa flour into the dough until it is not sticky.
4. Place onto a baking tray lined with parchment paper and flatten into a flatbread shape (round like a biscuit) that

is ½ inch thick and about 3 inches in diameter.

5. Bake at 400 degrees F for about 25 minutes, until light golden in color.

. . . .

Butters

TIP: It is helpful to soak and dehydrate seeds and to keep them stored in the freezer until you use them for recipes like these.

*TIP: When processing seed butters, it is helpful to **not** add salt until the end of processing. Adding salt too early will greatly lengthen processing time*

COCONUT/PUMPKIN SEED BUTTER

Ingredients:

- 1 cup dehydrated coconut flakes
- 1 cup pumpkin seeds, soaked and dehydrated
- ½ teaspoon unrefined salt, or to taste (add when the butter is nearly done processing)

Directions:

1. Process in a food processor for about 20 minutes until a nice spreadable consistency.
2. Add salt towards the end of processing

Note: The shredded coconut in this recipe will cause the butter harden when stored in the refrigerator. Let it soften at room temperature prior to eating.

COCONUT/SUNFLOWER SEED BUTTER

Ingredients:

- 1 cup dehydrated coconut flakes
- 1 cup sunflower seeds, soaked and dehydrated.
- ½ teaspoon unrefined salt, or to taste (add toward the end of processing)

Directions:

1. Process in a food processor for about 20 minutes until you achieve a nice, spreadable consistency.
2. Add salt towards the end of processing.

Note: The shredded coconut in this recipe will cause the butter harden when stored in the refrigerator. Let it soften at room temperature prior to eating.

PUMPKIN SEED BUTTER

Ingredients:

- 2 cups pumpkin seeds, soaked and dehydrated. *Seeds must be fully dehydrated for this recipe*
- ½ teaspoon unrefined salt, or to taste (add towards the end of processing)

Directions:

1. Place in a food processor and process for about 20 minutes until it reaches a nice, spreadable consistency.

2. Add salt towards the end of processing.
3. Serve with flatbread and honey to sweeten.

SUNFLOWER SEED BUTTER

Ingredients:

- 2 cups sunflower seeds, soaked and dehydrated. *Seeds have to be fully dehydrated for this recipe.*
- ½ teaspoon unrefined salt, or to taste (add towards the end of processing)

Directions:

1. Process in a food processor for about 20 minutes until you achieve a nice spreadable consistency.
2. Add salt towards the end of processing.

3. Serve with flatbread and honey to sweeten.

SIDE OF STUFFED AVOCADO WITH SALSA

This makes an attractive alternative to plain old avocado.

Ingredients:

- 2 avocados
- 2 teaspoons fresh squeezed lemon juice
- ⅛ teaspoon salt

Directions:

1. Cut avocados in half.
2. Remove the pit and carefully scoop out the pulp of the avocado, leaving a thin rim around the inside of the shell.
3. Place the pulp into a mixing bowl.
4. Mash the pulp with a fork and add fresh lemon juice and salt to taste.
5. Spoon the avocado pulp back into the halves.
6. Top the halves with salsa (see below) and eat as you would guacamole.

SALSA

Ingredients:

- 1 cup packed fresh cilantro (leaves and stems), chopped finely
- 4 fresh basil leaves, chopped finely
- ¼ cup finely chopped onion, approximately ½ small onion
- 1 clove garlic, pressed or minced
- 1 teaspoon unrefined salt
- 3 cups fresh tomatoes, diced
- Pinch of cayenne pepper (optional)

Directions:

1. Ingredients may be prepared individually or together in food processor. For food processor, chop the cilantro and basil finely before placing it in the food processor.
2. Process all the ingredients except the tomatoes to a finely chopped consistency. Coarsely chop tomatoes before adding to processor. Process lightly until the tomatoes are at your preferred consistency. Transfer into a serving bowl.

PESTO PERFECTO

Serve with raw spiralized zucchini noodles, baked sweet potatoes, or potatoes.

Ingredients:

- 1 cup sunflower seeds, soaked overnight and rinsed
- 1 handful spinach
- ½ cup fresh basil

- 2 green onions
- 1 tablespoon freshly squeezed lemon
- ¼ red bell pepper
- 1 clove garlic
- ½ cup water

Directions:

1. Blend all ingredients and serve.

SWEET POTATO NON-FRIES

Ingredients:

- 2 sweet potatoes, (we like the Asian variety)
- ¼ teaspoon cardamom
- ¼ teaspoon coriander
- 1 tablespoon flaxseed
- 2 teaspoons shredded coconut
- Unrefined salt sprinkled to taste

Directions:

1. Place a steamer basket into a medium sized sauce pan and fill with 1-2 inches of water.
2. Chop the sweet potatoes into wedges that resemble thick fries.
3. Place the sweet potatoes into the steamer basket, cover and bring water to a boil. Once boiling, lower the heat and simmer for about 25 minutes, until sweet potatoes are soft but still have good form.
4. Mix the rest of the ingredients together in a small bowl.
5. When the potatoes are done steaming, drain the water and place them into a medium-sized mixing bowl.
6. Sprinkle the seasoning mixture over the potatoes and mix well so the sweet

potatoes are coated.

7. Line a baking tray with parchment paper and place the wedges on the tray. Bake at 400 degrees for 15 minutes.

8. Flip the wedges and bake for another 15 minutes.

STEAMED PURPLE SWEET POTATOES

A beautiful simple dish that can be used in place of Yuca on day two of our meal plan. Purple sweet potatoes add a wonderful splash of color to any meal.

Ingredients:

* 4 purple sweet potatoes, whole and unpeeled

Directions:

1. Place in a steamer basket and steam until thoroughly cooked, approximately 40 minute.

Servings: 4
Prep time: 5 minutes
Cook time: 40 minutes

MEXICAN VEGGIE MEAT

This recipe can be used in the veggie wrap or tortilla. It can be used in any recipe that might call for a chewy, savory, and veggie meat type of ingredient. It requires dehydration, so it needs to

be made in advance. It can easily be packed for lunches, as it travels well!*

Ingredients:

* 2 cups sunflower seeds, soaked 8 hours and rinsed
* 5 cups zucchini, shredded
* 1/2 cup onion, minced
* 1 cup celery, minced
* 1/2 cup homemade chili powder
* 1/4 cup lemon juice
* 1 teaspoon unrefined salt
* 2 garlic cloves, crushed

Directions:

1. Use a food processor to process sunflower seeds into a flour.
2. In a large bowl, combine with other ingredients.
3. Spread the mixture onto two dehydrator sheets lined with parchment paper.
4. Dehydrate at 109 degrees F for 5 hours (or until it reaches your desired consistency).

CREAMY ZUCCHINI SANDWICH SPREAD

This spread is rich in fat and flavor and provides lots of fresh, raw veggies!

Vegetable ingredients:

* 1 cup sunflower seeds, soaked 8 hours and rinsed

- 1 medium zucchini
- 2 stalks celery
- 3 green onion, thinly sliced
- ¼ small onion, diced
- 2 tablespoons dried dill

Dressing Ingredients:

- Meat of 1 young coconut
- ¾ cup young coconut water
- 2 cloves garlic
- ¼ cup lemon juice
- 1 teaspoon unrefined salt
- ½ cup sunflower seeds, soaked overnight and rinsed

Directions:

1. Pulse sunflower seeds in food processor until crumbly.
2. Place into a mixing bowl.
3. Cut zucchini, celery and onion into medium sized pieces before placing all the ingredients in a food processor and process until the final product is finely chopped (but not overly done or liquefied).
4. Combine the vegetables with sunflower seeds and mix well.
5. Blend all the dressing ingredients until creamy.
6. Pour the dressing over the salad, and toss to mix well.
7. Chill 1-2 hours before serving.

Raw Crackers

SUNFLOWER SEED CRACKERS

Ingredients:

- 1 cup flax seeds
- 1 cup water
- 4 cups sunflower seeds soaked
- ½ large carrot to make 1 cup of finely processed carrot
- 1 cup water
- 2 tablespoons dried dill or rosemary
- 1 teaspoon salt

Directions:

1. In a large mixing bowl, soak flaxseed with 1 cup water for 1 hour.
2. In a food processor, process sunflower seeds until they are coarsely chopped, but not overly processed.
3. Add processed seeds to the mixing bowl.

95

4. Process ½ a large carrot to a fine consistency and add it to the mixing bowl.
5. Add water, dill or rosemary, and salt. Mix well.
6. Line dehydrator trays with parchment paper and place the mixture on dehydrator trays, spreading the mixture well so that there is a thin, continuous layer over the entire tray.
7. Use a butter knife to score this into cracker sized pieces.
8. Dehydrate for about 18 hours at 109 degrees F, until completely dried.
9. Top with honey and enjoy at breakfast. Delicious!

FLAXSEED CRACKERS

Ingredients:

- 2 cups flax seeds (soaked for 1-2 hours in 2 cups of water)
- ⅓ cup red bell pepper, chopped finely
- ⅔ cup sun dried tomatoes
- ⅓ cup fresh cilantro or basil, chopped finely
- 1 ¼ cups tomatoes, diced
- 1 clove garlic, minced
- Pinch cayenne
- 1 teaspoon unrefined salt

Directions:

1. Place bell pepper, cilantro, sun dried tomatoes, tomatoes, cayenne , garlic, and salt into food processor and process until pureed.

2. Transfer contents into a large bowl and mix in the flax seeds.
3. Spread mixture onto a dehydrator sheet and dehydrate at 109 degrees F for about 18 hours.

BUCKWHEAT CRACKERS

Ingredients:

- 1½ cups raw buckwheat groats, sprouted 2 days and rinsed
- 1 small bell pepper
- ½ zucchini
- 1 cup of young coconut meat. (This requires 1-2 young coconuts)
- ½ teaspoon unrefined salt.
- 1 teaspoon dried basil (optional)
- ¼ teaspoon dried oregano (optional)

Directions:

1. Pulse buckwheat groats in food processor. The groats should be coarsely chopped and not overly processed.
2. Place the processed groats into a large bowl.
3. Quarter the bell pepper and cut zucchini into smaller pieces before placing into processor.
4. In the food processor, pulse the bell pepper and zucchini into finely chopped pieces (doing your best not to puree the mixture) and add it to the bowl when done.
5. Process coconut meat very thoroughly and add it to the bowl.

6. Mix all ingredients well.
7. Spread onto dehydrator trays lined with parchment paper.
8. Dehydrate at 109 degrees F for about 18 hours. Crackers should be very dry without a hint of moisture or softness.
9. Use in place of bread for lunch.
10. Top with avocado slices and a pinch of salt.

. . . .

Wraps, Tortillas

BELL PEPPER VEGGIE WRAPS

These wraps can be served with lettuce, veggie cream, avocado and salsa.

Ingredients:

- 6 cups chopped red bell pepper
- 4 cups chopped tomatoes
- 2 tsp salt
- 1 small avocado
- ½ cup flaxseed, ground

Directions:

1. Blend peppers, tomatoes, and salt.
2. Add avocado and continue blending.
3. Add flaxseed.
4. Spread over parchment paper on a dehydrator tray into a thin layer.
5. Shape as tortillas.
6. Dehydrate at 109 degrees F for 5-6 hrs.
7. Then flip over for 4 hours.
8. Wraps should be dry but still very pliable.

QUINOA TORTILLAS

This recipe takes some time to make but they are worth the effort. The tortillas can be made early in the week, frozen, and then used for packed lunches, travel, and for meal planning. They are super tasty too!

Ingredients:

- 2 medium potatoes, unpeeled
- 1 cup arrowroot powder, plus more for rolling
- 1 cup sprouted quinoa flour
- 1 ½ teaspoons flaxseed, ground
- 1 ½ teaspoons guar gum
- 1 teaspoon unrefined salt

Directions:

1. Place whole potatoes into a steamer basket and saucepan with approximately 1 inch of water at the bottom of the saucepan. Cover the saucepan.
2. Bring water to a boil and then lower heat to simmer until tender, about 20 minutes.
3. Drain fluid and remove potatoes from saucepan.
4. Cut potatoes so that they fill a measuring cup and measure 1½ cup to use for recipe.
5. Place potatoes in a food processor with the remaining ingredients and process until a dough is formed. The dough should not be sticky; add quinoa flour until the dough is soft, pliable, and does not stick to your hands.

6. When the dough is well blended, spoon it into your hand and form into small balls, approximately 2 inches in diameter
7. Use a tortilla press (lined with waxed paper or plastic) to press the dough ball into a flat tortilla. If no tortilla press is available, roll the dough into thin circles, dusting lightly with arrowroot flour to prevent sticking.
8. Place the tortillas in a heated cast iron or ceramic skillet for about 1 minute, turn over with spatula and toast until light golden brown on both sides.
9. Use them as you would use a tortilla or taco.

• • • • • • • • • • • • • • • • • • • •

Chips

KALE CHIPS

These kale chips are processed at a low enough temperature so that they will still have enzymes and bacteria to help repopulate your gut. They contain no nuts, no yeast and no vinegars. Best of all, they taste great!

Ingredients:

- 2 large bunches of kale, remove stems and thick ribs

Marinade:

- 1 ½ cups sunflower seeds, soaked overnight

- 1 cup water
- ¼ cup freshly squeezed lemon juice
- ½ red bell pepper
- 1 tablespoon honey
- 1 teaspoon unrefined salt
- 2 teaspoons onion powder
- 1 clove garlic
- Dash ground cayenne pepper
- 1 teaspoon dill

Directions:

1. Blend marinade ingredients until smooth.
2. Let the mixture stand in the refrigerator for at least one hour or ideally overnight.
3. Remove the long stems that run up through the kale leaves and tear the kale into medium-large pieces.
4. In a large container, mix the kale leaves in with the marinade. Thoroughly cover each leaf, mixing and massaging by hand.
5. Spread leaves on solid dehydrator trays in a single layer.
6. Dehydrate at 109°F for about 18 hours, or until dry and crisp.

ZUCCHINI CHIPS

Slicing the zucchini lengthwise will speed up the time it takes to marinate the zucchini. Use a mandoline to thinly slice the zucchini.

Ingredients:

- 2 medium-size zucchinis, thinly sliced lengthwise

- 1 tablespoon lemon juice
- 1 tablespoon water
- ½ teaspoon garlic powder
- 1 teaspoon onion powder
- ½ teaspoon paprika
- ½ teaspoon salt
- Dash cayenne pepper
- 2 tablespoons ground flaxseed

Directions:

1. Mix all ingredients well until the zucchini is well coated.
2. Place a single layer of zucchini on each tray (avoid overlapping).
3. Dehydrate for 18 hours at 109F.
4. Will store 1 month in an airtight container.

ONION RINGS

These crunchy onion rings provide a nice side to sandwiches, potatoes, legumes and salad.

Ingredients:

- 2 large yellow onions
- 1 ½ cups sprouted buckwheat flour
- 1 tablespoon Super Antioxidant Seasoning
- 1 cup of meat of 1 young coconut
- ½ cup water
- ½ teaspoon salt

Directions:

1. Cut the onions in half and then use a mandoline to make very thin onion

rings out of each onion half. Onion rings should be as thin as possible, yet still intact.
2. Set aside the onions and blend all other ingredients (except onion) together.
3. Coat the onion slices in mixture until well combined.
4. Spread out over dehydrator trays lined with parchment paper.
5. Dehydrate at 109 degrees F for about 24 hours.

. . . .

Vegetable Patties

VEGGIE BEAN PATTY

This patty makes a great tasting sandwich with our flat bread recipe.

Ingredients:

- 1 cup black beans, soaked overnight
- ½ onion
- 1 stalk celery
- ½ teaspoon unrefined salt
- 1 medium-sized potato
- 1 cup sunflower seeds, soaked overnight
- ¾ cups medium onion, chopped
- ¼ cup ground flax seed
- 2 cloves garlic, finely minced
- 1 tablespoon dried cilantro
- 1 tablespoon Super Antioxidant Seasoning
- ½ teaspoon unrefined salt, or to taste

Directions:

1. Soak black beans and sunflower seeds overnight.
2. Rinse before cooking.
3. Place beans, ½ onion, and celery in sauce pan and cover with enough water so that the water level is approximately 1 inch over the level of the beans.
4. Cook for one hour, or until soft.
5. Add salt and cook for 5 minutes more.
6. Cook or steam potato for approximately 20 minutes or until tender.
7. In a food processor, process the sunflower seeds and beans together.
8. Place in a large mixing bowl.
9. Then process or manually mash potato until mashed potato consistency. Add to the mixing bowl.
10. Add ¾ chopped onion, minced garlic, flaxseed, cilantro, Super Antioxidant Seasoning, and salt.
11. Use the lid of a small mouthed canning jar to form the patties. Place the patties on a parchment paper lined baking tray.
12. Bake at 375 degrees F for 20 minutes. Turn patties over and bake for an additional 10 minutes or until lightly golden.

Makes: 14 patties
Prep time: 20 minutes
Cook time: Beans 1 hour, Patties 30 minutes

Garbanzo Patty

This patty has a nice, nutty flavor from sunflower seeds and a crunch from buckwheat groats. It is good for sandwiches or can be eaten with a gravy sauce and mashed potatoes.

Ingredients:

Beans:

- 1 cup garbanzo beans, soaked overnight
- ½ onion
- 1 celery stalk
- ½ teaspoon unrefined salt, add at the end of cooking time

Quinoa-Buckwheat:

- ½ cup quinoa, soaked overnight
- ½ cup buckwheat groats, soaked overnight
- ½ teaspoon unrefined salt
- 2 cups sunflower seeds, soaked overnight
- 1 cup onion, chopped coarsely (may do in food processor)
- 4 cloves of garlic, minced
- ½-1 teaspoon unrefined salt, to taste
- ¼ cup ground flax seed
- 2 tablespoons Super Antioxidant Seasoning (Optional, see index for recipe)

Directions:

1. Soak garbanzo beans, quinoa, buckwheat and sunflower seeds overnight.
2. Place beans, onions, and celery in sauce pan and cover with enough water so that the water level is approximately 1 inch over the level of the beans.
3. Cook for one hour, or until soft.
4. Add salt and cook for 5 minutes more.
5. Place quinoa, buckwheat, and ½ teaspoon salt into a saucepan with 1 cup of water and bring to boil.
6. Simmer for approximately 15 minutes.
7. In a food processor, pulse the beans until they are finely processed (not a cream) and place in a large mixing bowl.
8. Pulse the sunflower seeds until finely processed and place in the with bowl with beans.
9. Process the quinoa and buckwheat in the processor until finely processed. Place this into the mixing bowl as well.
10. Add the garlic, 1 teaspoon unrefined salt, ground flaxseed and chopped onion to the processed ingredients and mix well.
11. Use the lid of a small-mouthed canning jar to form the patties.
12. Line a baking tray with parchment paper and place the patties on the lined tray.
13. Bake at 375 degrees F for 30 minutes. Turn patties over and bake an additional 15 minutes.

Makes: 28 patties
Prep time: 20 minutes
Cook time: Beans 1 hour, Patties 45 minutes

Lentil Patty

This patty is very simple to make and has a wonderful flavor. As with all the patties, it is great for sandwiches, or eating as a side with gravy and mashed potatoes.

Ingredients:

Lentils:

- 1 cup brown lentils, soaked overnight
- 2 teaspoons onion powder
- 1 teaspoon garlic powder
- ½ teaspoon salt
- 1 cup sunflower seeds, soaked overnight
- 1 zucchini
- 1 tablespoon onion powder
- 1 teaspoon garlic powder
- 1 tablespoon Super Antioxidant Seasoning
- ¼ cup of ground flax seed

Directions:

1. Place lentils, onion powder, and garlic powder in a saucepan and cover with enough water so that the water level is approximately 1 inch over the level of the lentils.
2. Bring water to a boil and then lower heat to simmer for approximately 30 min, or until lentils are soft.
3. Add salt and cook 5 minutes more.
4. Process sunflower seeds finely and place them in a mixing bowl.
5. Process zucchini finely, then manually squeeze out all excess fluid from the processed zucchini.
6. Use your hands or nut milk bag to do this.
7. Add the zucchini to the sunflower seeds in the mixing bowl with 1 tablespoon of onion powder, 1 teaspoon garlic powder, 1 tablespoon Super Antioxidant Seasoning and ground flax seed.
8. Use a colander to strain the cooked lentils and then add the lentils to the mixing bowl.
9. Mix all the ingredients well.
10. Line a baking tray with parchment paper.
11. Use the lid of a small-mouthed canning jar to form the patties and place the patties on the lined tray.
12. Bake at 375 degrees for 20 minutes, turn the patties, and bake an additional 10 minutes, or until browned.

Prep time: 15-20 minutes
Cook time: 30 minutes lentils
Bake time: 30 minutes

Salads

Red Cabbage Salad

This is a beautifully colorful salad that provides a small amount of cabbage, a member of the cruciferous family.

Ingredients:

- ½ head red lettuce
- ½ cup shredded red cabbage
- ¼ cup shredded carrot
- ½ onion, sliced thinly and marinated in 1 tablespoon fresh lemon juice
- 2 medium-sized tomatoes, sliced thinly
- ½ cup green onion, chopped finely
- 1 tablespoon freshly squeezed lemon juice
- ⅛ teaspoon salt

You may add any or all of the following:

- ½ cup parsley, chopped finely
- 1 sliced avocado, if not using avocado dressing
- ½ cucumber, sliced finely
- 2 tablespoons fresh dill, or sprinkled dried dill

Directions:

1. Marinate sliced onion in lemon juice and salt for about 30 minutes. Toss ingredients and mix well with dressing of choice.

Serves: 4

Mixed Green Salad

Radishes are another member of the cruciferous family. They provide helpful enzymes, like myrosinase, that unlock the cancer fighting properties of broccoli and others that can protect the liver against various toxins!

Ingredients:

- ½ head of romaine lettuce
- 4 radishes, chopped finely
- 2 cups spinach, packed
- 2 tomatoes, diced
- ⅓ cucumber, in thin half slices
- ½ onion, sliced very thin
- 1 tablespoon freshly squeezed lemon juice
- ⅛ teaspoon unrefined salt

Directions:

1. Marinate sliced onion and radish in lemon juice and salt for about 30 minutes.
2. Toss ingredients and mix well with dressing of choice.

Serves: 4

Garden Salad

A basic salad that provides lots of flavor, healing vitamins, and minerals.

Ingredients:

- ½ head red lettuce, torn or chopped into bite-sized pieces
- ½ head romaine lettuce, torn or chopped into bite-sized pieces

- 4 green onions, chopped finely
- 2 small tomatoes, diced
- 1 radish, sliced very thin
- ⅓ cucumber, sliced very thin
- ½ red onion, sliced very thin
- 1 tablespoon freshly squeezed lemon juice
- ¼ teaspoon unrefined salt

Directions:

1. Use a mandoline to slice red onion into very thin slices and marinate in lemon juice and salt for about 30 minutes before adding to the salad. (You may use mandoline to slice the radish and cucumber as well).
2. Combine all the ingredients into a large mixing bowl and mix well with your dressing of choice, just before serving.

Serves: 4

- ¼ bell pepper, diced
- ¼ tomato, diced
- ½ avocado
- ¼ onion, finely sliced
  1 tablespoon freshly squeezed lemon juice
- ⅛ teaspoon unrefined salt, or to taste

Directions:

1. Finely slice the onion using a mandoline and marinate the onion pieces in a small dish with lemon juice and salt.
2. Prepare the rest of the salad ingredients and toss together.
3. Cut the avocado into small pieces and mix well with the other ingredients.
4. If you're packing for lunch, pack the marinated onion in a separate container and combine with avocado and salad only when you are ready to eat.

Prep time: 15 minutes

SALAD FOR ONE

Just in case you're not prepping for a family, here is a salad for one!

Ingredients:

- 2 leaves of green leafy lettuce, torn or chopped into bite-sized pieces
- 2 leaves of romaine lettuce, torn or chopped into bite-sized pieces
- 1 green onion, chopped finely
- ¼ cucumber in thin half slices
- ¼ small carrot grated

QUINOA SALAD

Quinoa salad is so easy, so tasty, and such a great way to get your high energy seeds and veggies!

Ingredients:

- ½ cup quinoa, soaked overnight and rinsed
- 1 teaspoon onion powder
- ¼ teaspoon garlic powder
- ¼ teaspoon salt
- 1 cup tomato, diced

- ¼ cup green onion, sliced
- 1 large radish sliced
- ¼ cup yellow bell pepper, chopped
- ½ romaine lettuce, chopped
- 1 large avocado, diced
- 1 tablespoon lemon juice

Directions:

1. Cook quinoa with 1 cup of water added onion, garlic, and salt, cook for about 15 minutes, until all water is absorbed.
2. Cool quinoa, add the rest of ingredients, and mix well.

· ·

Salad Dressings

AVOCADO DRESSING

So simple and so flavorful!

Ingredients:

- 2 avocados
- 1 tablespoon freshly squeezed lemon juice
- ¾ cup water
- ½ teaspoon unrefined salt or to taste

Directions:

1. Mash the avocados and mix together with the other ingredients until creamy.
2. Mix well with salad prior to serving. It gives a wonderful flavor.

CREAMY SUNFLOWER DRESSING

Ingredients:

- ¼ cup sunflower seeds, soaked overnight and rinsed
- 1 teaspoon salt
- 2 teaspoons lemon juice
- ½ teaspoon onion powder
- ¼ teaspoon garlic powder
- ¼ tsp honey
- 1 cup water

Directions:

1. Blend the above until creamy.
2. Refrigerate unused dressing for up to three days.

TOMATO LEMON HERB DRESSING

Ingredients:

- 2 tablespoons lemon
- 1 large peeled tomato, 1 cup
- ¼ teaspoon honey
- ¼ teaspoon unrefined salt
- ¼ teaspoon dill
- ¼ teaspoon of garlic powder

Directions:

1. Blend well and serve
2. Makes approximately ½ cup dressing

Cheeses, Sauces, and Gravy

Taco Cheese

Serve with crackers, tortillas, veggie wraps, as a dip for veggies, or for bread and sandwiches.

Ingredients:

- 1 cup sunflower seeds, soaked overnight
- ½ cup water
- 2 tablespoons freshly squeezed lemon juice
- ¼ red bell pepper (about ¼ cup)
- 1 tsp honey
- ½ teaspoon unrefined salt
- 1 tsp onion powder
- ¼ teaspoon garlic powder
- Dash ground cayenne pepper
- ½ teaspoon dill

Directions:

- Blend all ingredients until smooth.

Vegan Cheese Melt

Use as a topping for potatoes, sweet potatoes, patties, or veggie pizza.

Ingredients:

- 1 cup Quick Coconut Milk
- 2 tablespoons arrowroot powder
- 1 small clove garlic
- ¾ teaspoon salt
- 1 teaspoon lemon juice

Directions:

1. ¼ cup sunflower seeds, soaked overnight. (Optional: using sunflower seeds makes the cheese richer, but it is possible to make without it).
2. Blend all the ingredients until creamy and pour into a small saucepan.
3. Bring to a boil over low heat, stirring constantly.

Coconaise

This is a sour cream or mayonnaise substitute that can be used for sandwiches, tacos, potatoes, and sweet potatoes. Making fresh coconut milk is the time limiting factor. Consider using this recipe if you are making coconut milk for breakfast and you have some left over!

Ingredients:

- 1 cup fresh coconut milk
- Meat of 1 young coconut
- ½ clove garlic
- ½ teaspoon onion powder
- 1 tablespoon lemon juice
- ½ teaspoon salt

Directions:

1. Blend well until creamy. Store covered in refrigerator and use within 3 days.

COUNTRY STYLE GRAVY

Use with mashed potatoes and veggie patties.

Ingredients:

- 2 cups water
- ½ cup sunflower seeds, soaked overnight
- 1 tablespoon onion powder
- ¼ teaspoon garlic powder
- ½ teaspoon salt
- 1 tablespoon Super Antioxidant Seasoning (see index)
- 1 tablespoon arrowroot powder

Directions:

1. Blend all ingredients until creamy.
2. Pour into saucepan and cook over medium heat until thick, stirring constantly.

. . . .

Seasonings

SUPER ANTIOXIDANT SEASONING

Ingredients:

- 12 tablespoons dried parsley
- 4 tablespoons onion powder
- 1 tablespoon Real salt
- 2 tablespoons dried sage
- 2 tablespoons dried thyme
- 2 tablespoons garlic powder
- 1 tablespoon dried marjoram
- 1 tablespoon dried dill weed
- ½ teaspoon paprika
- ½ teaspoon rosemary
- 1 teaspoon basil
- ½ teaspoon oregano, optional

Directions:

1. Mix or blend all ingredients together in blender.
2. Store in airtight container (refrigeration optional).

CHILI POWDER

Ingredients:

- 1 cup paprika powder
- 2 tablespoons oregano
- 2 tablespoons unrefined salt
- 5 tablespoons cumin powder
- 5 tablespoons garlic powder

Directions

1. Mix or blend the above.
2. Store in an airtight container away from light and moisture.

. . . .

Dessert

You will want to significantly limit sugar intake during phase 1 of healing; this includes fruit sugars. Use these recipes sparingly when you are in phase 2 of healing.

Raw Key Lime Pie

Recipes like these are good reasons to soak, dehydrate, and freeze larger quantities of sunflower and pumpkin seeds to have on hand. If you are in a pinch, perhaps you can purchase sunflower and pumpkin seeds that have already been soaked and dehydrated, as it will speed up the process of making the crust. Or you can simply make the filling and eat it on its own as a pudding. It's quite delicious that way as well. Don't eat too much or too often, as it is quite sweet!

Filling ingredients:

- 5 medium-sized avocados
- Meat of 2 young coconuts
- ¾ cup coconut water
- ¼ cup plus 2 tablespoons freshly squeezed lime juice
- 2 tablespoons vanilla
- ½ teaspoon unrefined salt
- 1 cup raw honey
- 1 teaspoon stevia leaf herb (ground whole leaf powder)
- 1 teaspoon ground flax seed
- ¼ cup dehydrated coconut flakes

Crust ingredients:

- 1 cup sunflower seed, soaked and dehydrated
- 1 cup pumpkin seed, soaked and dehydrated
- 1 tablespoon carob powder
- 2 teaspoons raw honey
- ½ teaspoon vanilla
- ⅛ teaspoon unrefined salt

- ¼ teaspoon stevia (ground whole leaf powder) (optional)

Directions:

1. Process all the crust ingredients in a food processor until the mixture sticks together and will press easily.
2. Press into a pie plate and chill.
3. Blend all filling ingredients (except dried coconut) in a blender until smooth and creamy.
4. Pour filling into crust and chill for a few hours.
5. Sprinkle shredded coconut on top.

Pumpkin Pie

Filling Ingredients:

- 2 cups pumpkin (1 small pumpkin)
- 1 cup meat of a young Thai coconut (1-2 coconuts)
- ½ cup honey
- ½ cup sunflower seed
- 1 tablespoon vanilla
- ½ teaspoon cardamom
- ½ teaspoon coriander
- Pinch of ginger powder
- 2 teaspoons ground flax meal (optional, to thicken)
- 1 tablespoon Maple Syrup

Crust Ingredients:

- 1 cup sunflower seeds
- 1 cup pumpkin seeds
- 2 teaspoons honey

- 1 teaspoon vanilla

Directions for filling:

1. Cut the pumpkin in half, remove the seeds.
2. Place the pumpkin halves in a steamer basket with 2 inches of water in a saucepan.
3. Steam for about 20-25 minutes, until the pumpkin is tender when tested with a fork.
4. When done, scoop out the orange flesh and pack into 2 cups.
5. Place into the blender.
6. Open the young coconut (*save the coconut water for a delicious drink!*).
7. For the pie, scoop out enough of the fleshy white meat to pack one cup tightly; add to blender.
8. Add the rest of the ingredients to the blender and blend until smooth.

Directions for crust:

1. Process sunflower and pumpkin seeds by themselves for a few minutes until the mixture becomes sticky and starts forming a ball, or sticks to the sides of the container. You may need to stop occasionally to scrape down the sides of the processor. Keep processing until the seeds are all processed.
2. Add honey and vanilla.
3. Process it until the mixture is sticky enough so that it will stick to the pan. It is okay if it is granular.

Putting it together:

1. Remove the crust mixture from the processor and press into a pie pan.
2. Pour in the contents of the blender into the pie pan.
3. Glaze the top of pie with Maple syrup to give it a darker, more traditional appearance.
4. Refrigerate or place in freezer for about 30 minutes if you are serving it right away. You can also keep the pie in the freezer and remove it about an hour before serving.

PART V

BECOMING WHOLE

WHOLENESS AND THE 9 LAWS OF HEALTH

We believe that positive thoughts and lifestyle choices are just as critical to your health as nutrition. Read through these laws of health to see how well you are preparing yourself to live a happy, healthy, and whole life.

W—Water intake. Drink purified, filtered water. Unpurified water may contain fluoride, chlorine, and residues of pharmaceutical drugs. Drink water first thing in the morning and throughout the day, and not at meals so you don't dilute hydrochloric acid. A rule of thumb: divide your weight in pounds in half, and drink that many ounces of water daily.

H—Establish **Habits** of regularity in your daily activities and make a habit of avoiding addictive substances.

O—Oxygen. Get outside to get fresh air on a daily basis. Practice having good posture and good breathing practices to fully expand your lungs. Breathing well at night is important too, so make sure you are on the lookout for sleep disturbances such as sleep apnea or upper airway resistance syndrome.

L—Love. Examine your relationship with yourself, with God, and with others. Consider how you handle stress and if you struggle with bitterness, resentment, or fear. Do you have any traumatic events in your life that still cause you to react with raw emotions? These might indicate that these wounds have not healed and are causing symptoms whether or not you are aware of it.

E—Environment. Get rid of mold in your home or toxins in foods or cosmetics. Toxins, molds, and heavy metals have an even more powerful impact on chronic disease than nutrition.

N—Nutrition. What are the sources of inflammation in your diet? See our chapter on autoimmune disease for more information.

E—Exercise. Get regular physical activity every day.

S—Sleep. Sleep at regular hours, seven to eight hours a day. Getting a few hours of sleep before midnight improves melatonin production, which impacts the immune system.

S—Sunshine. Summertime exposure to sunlight is vital for vitamin D and other helpful benefits!

WHY PLANT-BASED?

Despite amazing advances in science and technology, there is ironically still much confusion about human nutrition. Whether you believe in a paleo or plant-based diet, there appears to be research that validates either philosophy. How can one know what to believe?

We believe that health is a byproduct of living according to the physiological laws of life These are immutable laws that govern how we live and how the universe functions. Through the systematic study of life—otherwise known as science—we understand that these laws cannot be broken. They simply explain how life works.

One of our guiding lights has been the belief that a loving Creator created humanity according to these laws and that He designed us for health. We therefore believe that these laws can be found in the Bible and can be validated through scientific observation. According to the Bible, a plant-based diet was the original diet given to mankind in Genesis. Scientific research validates that an organic, chemical free, highly mineralized, and plant based diet makes sense physiologically and ecologically.

Is it possible that there are forces at work to destroy trust in a loving Creator and that this disbelief causes us to live lives that are at odds with the laws of our nature? Is it possible that there is a Creator who has your very best interest at heart? We encourage you to have courage to believe. We believe that only He can bring healing and happiness into your life.

GLOSSARY

Dysbiosis is a condition in which one or more potentially harmful microbes are dominant.

GMOs the abbreviation for genetically modified organism. Genetic modification involves the mutation, insertion, or deletion of genes. Inserted genes usually come from a different species in a form of Horizontal gene-transfer.

Gut Microbiome refers to the community of microbes--bacteria, viruses, fungi--in the gut.

Normobiosis is a condition in which microbes with potential health benefits predominate in number over those which are potentially harmful and there is healthy balance.

RESOURCES

Healthy Shopping

azurestandard.com (Organic foods with convenient bulk order and distribution program)

spud.ca (Canadian organic produce)

purelivingorganic.com (Sprouted organic flours)

shilohfarms.com (Sprouted organic flours)

healthyflour.com (Sprouted organic flours)

thrivemarket.com (Sprouted organic flours)

sunfood.com (Dehydrated olives without additives)

Environmental Impact Resources

ewg.org (Education regarding chemicals used in household cleaning and cosmetics)

ENDNOTES

[1] How many Americans have an autoimmune disease? American Autoimmune Related Diseases Association, Inc. https://www.aarda.org/knowledge-base/many-americans-autoimmune-disease/. April 29,2017. [Accessed 21 February 2019].

[2] The Autoimmune Diseases Coordinating Committee. *Progress in Autoimmune Diseases Research*. https://www.niaid.nih.gov/sites/default/files/adccfinal.pdf. [Accessed 21 February 2019].

[3] Jamison, Dean T., et al., eds. *Disease control priorities in developing countries*. The World Bank, 2006.

[4] Skeldon, Alexander, and Maya Saleh. "The inflammasomes: molecular effectors of host resistance against bacterial, viral, parasitic, and fungal infections." *Frontiers in microbiology* 2 (2011): 15.

[5] WHO Guidelines for Indoor Air Quality; Dampness and Mould. World Health Organization. http://www.euro.who.int/__data/assets/pdf_file/0017/43325/E92645.pdf. [Accessed 21 February 2019].

[6] Tim Newman. Common chemicals in plastic linked to chronic disease. Medical news Today. https://www.medicalnewstoday.com/articles/318422.php. July 14, 2017. [Accessed 21 February 2019].

[7] Stejskal, Vera, Karin Öckert, and Geir Bjørklund. "Metal-induced inflammation triggers fibromyalgia in metal-allergic patients." *Neuroendocrinology Letters* 34.6 (2013): 559-65.

[8] Jon Johnson. What you should know about hair dye allergies. Medical News Today. https://www.medicalnewstoday.com/articles/320505.php. January 5, 2018. [Accessed 21 February 2019].

[9] Stacy Matthews. Common Cosmetics and Skin Inflammation. Seaside Medical. https://www.seasidemedicaltech.com/blogs/news/common-cosmetics-and-skin-inflammation. September 9, 2017. [Accessed 21 February 2019].

[10] Karussis, Dimitrios, and Panayiota Petrou. "The spectrum of post-vaccination inflammatory CNS demyelinating syndromes." *Autoimmunity reviews* 13.3 (2014): 215-224.

[11] Divani, Afshin A., et al. "Effect of oral and vaginal hormonal contraceptives on inflammatory blood biomarkers." *Mediators of inflammation* 2015 (2015).

[12] Vongpatanasin, Wanpen, et al. "Differential effects of oral versus transdermal estrogen replacement therapy on C-reactive protein in postmenopausal women." *Journal of the American College of Cardiology* 41.8 (2003): 1358-1363.

[13] Mary Jane Brown. Does Sugar Cause Inflammation in the Body? Healthline. https://www.healthline.com/nutrition/sugar-and-inflammation. November 12, 2017. [Accessed 21 February 2019].

[14] López-Alarcón, Mardia, et al. "Excessive refined carbohydrates and scarce micronutrients intakes increase inflammatory mediators and insulin resistance in prepubertal and pubertal obese children independently of obesity." *Mediators of inflammation* 2014 (2014).

[15] Sanchari Sinha Dutta. Foods that Drive Inflammation. News Medical Life Sciences. https://www.news-medical.net/health/Foods-that-Drive-Inflammation.aspx. Updated Jan. 21, 2019. [Accessed 21 February 2019].

[16] Sara Reardon. Food Preservatives linked to obesity and gut disease. Nature. https://www.nature.com/news/food-preservatives-linked-to-obesity-and-gut-disease-1.16984. February 25, 2015. [Accessed 21 February 2019].

[17] Liu, Yun-Zi, Yun-Xia Wang, and Chun-Lei Jiang. "Inflammation: the common pathway of stress-related diseases." *Frontiers in human neuroscience* 11 (2017): 316.

[18] O'Neil, Adrienne, et al. "Depression is a risk factor for incident coronary heart disease in women: An 18-year longitudinal study." *Journal of affective disorders* 196 (2016): 117-124.

[19] Mullington, Janet M., et al. "Sleep loss and inflammation." *Best practice & research Clinical endocrinology & metabolism* 24.5 (2010): 775-784.

[20] Ertek, Sibel, and Arrigo Cicero. "Impact of physical activity on inflammation: effects on cardiovascular disease risk and other inflammatory conditions." *Archives of medical science: AMS* 8.5 (2012): 794.

[21] Gorman, Shelley, et al. "Can skin exposure to sunlight prevent liver inflammation?." *Nutrients* 7.5 (2015): 3219-3239.

[22] Lung Inflammation, Oxidative Stress and Air Pollution. Intechopen.com. https://www.intechopen.com/books/lung-inflammation/lung-inflammation-oxidative-stress-and-air-pollution. May 14, 2014. [Accessed 21 February 2019].

[23] NIH Human Microbiome Project defines normal bacterial makeup of the body. National Institutes of Health. https://www.nih.gov/news-events/news-releases/nih-human-microbiome-project-defines-normal-bacterial-makeup-body. June 13, 2012. [Accessed 2 September 2018].

[24] El-Matary, Wael, Karine Dupuis, and AbdulRazaq Sokoro. "Anti-S accharomyces cerevisiae antibody titres correlate well with disease activity in children with Crohn's disease." *Acta Paediatrica* 104.8 (2015): 827-830.

[25] Neuman, Hadar, and Omry Koren. "The gut microbiota: a possible factor influencing systemic lupus erythematosus." *Current opinion in rheumatology* 29.4 (2017): 374-377.

[26] Sakkas, Lazaros I., and Dimitrios P. Bogdanos. "Multiple hit infection and autoimmunity: the dysbiotic microbiota–ACPA connection in rheumatoid arthritis." *Current opinion in rheumatology* 30.4 (2018): 403-409.

[27] Rajca, Sylvie, et al. "Alterations in the intestinal microbiome (dysbiosis) as a predictor of relapse after infliximab withdrawal in Crohn's disease." *Inflammatory bowel diseases* 20.6 (2014): 978-986.

[28] Arrieta, M. C., L. Bistritz, and J. B. Meddings. "Alterations in intestinal permeability." *Gut* 55.10 (2006): 1512-1520.

[29] Fasano, Alessio. "Leaky gut and autoimmune diseases." *Clinical reviews in allergy & immunology* 42.1 (2012): 71-78.

[30] Lerner, Aaron, Yehuda Shoenfeld, and Torsten Matthias. "Adverse effects of gluten ingestion and advantages of gluten withdrawal in nonceliac autoimmune disease." *Nutrition reviews* 75.12 (2017): 1046-1058.

[31] Hollon, Justin, et al. "Effect of gliadin on permeability of intestinal biopsy explants from celiac disease patients and patients with non-celiac gluten sensitivity." *Nutrients* 7.3 (2015): 1565-1576.

[32] Losurdo, Giuseppe, et al. "Extra-intestinal manifestations of non-celiac gluten sensitivity: An expanding paradigm." *World journal of gastroenterology* 24.14 (2018): 1521.

[33] Van den Broeck, Hetty C., et al. "Presence of celiac disease epitopes in modern and old hexaploid wheat varieties: wheat breeding may have contributed to increased prevalence of celiac disease." *Theoretical and applied genetics* 121.8 (2010): 1527-15

[34] Thomas, David. "A Study on the Mineral Depletion of the Foods Available to Us as a Nation over the Period 1940 to 1991." *Nutrition and Health*, vol. 17, no. 2, Apr. 2003, pp. 85–115.

[35] Wallinga, David. "Today's Food System: How Healthy Is It?" *Journal of hunger & environmental nutrition* vol. 4,3-4 (2009): 251-281.

[36] Vrain, Thierry. "A former GMO scientist sends an open letter to Canada's minister of health." https://robynobrien.com/a-former-gmo-scientist-sends-an-open-letter-to-canadas-minister-of-health/. [Accessed 22 February 2019].

[37] Glyphosate Overview. GMO Free USA. https://gmofreeusa.org/research/glyphosate/glyphosate-overview/. [Accessed 22 February 2019].

[38] Samsel, Anthony, and Stephanie Seneff. "Glyphosate, pathways to modern diseases II: Celiac sprue and gluten intolerance." *Interdisciplinary toxicology* 6.4 (2013): 159-184.

[39] McKenzie, H et al. "Antibody to selected strains of Saccharomyces cerevisiae (baker's and brewer's yeast) and Candida albicans in Crohn's disease" *Gut* vol. 31,5 (1990): 536-8.

[40] Leff, Jonathan W., and Noah Fierer. "Bacterial communities associated with the surfaces of fresh fruits and vegetables." *PloS one* 8.3 (2013): e59310.

[41] Alex Formuzis. Roundup for Breakfast, Part 2: In New Tests, Weed Killer Found in All Kids' Cereals Sampled. EWG. https://www.ewg.org/release/roundup-breakfast-part-2-new-tests-weed-killer-found-all-kids-cereals-sampled. October 24, 2018. [Accessed 22 February 2019]

[42] Bishehsari, Faraz, et al. "Dietary fiber treatment corrects the composition of gut microbiota, promotes SCFA production, and suppresses colon carcinogenesis." *Genes* 9.2 (2018): 102.

[43] Amy Brown. "Lupus erythematosus and nutrition: A review of the literature." *Journal of Renal Nutrition*, 2000 Oct;10(4):170-83.

[44] Montanaro A, EJ Bardana Jr. "Dietary amino acid-induced systemic lupus erythematosus." *Rheum Dis Clin North Am.* 1991 May;17(2):323-32.

[45] Lee Alice, and Victoria Werth. "Activation of Autoimmunity Following Use of Immunostimulatory Herbal Supplements." *Arch Dermatol.* 2004;140(6):723–727.

[46] Tuohy, Kieran M., et al. "Up-regulating the human intestinal microbiome using whole plant foods, polyphenols, and/or fiber." *Journal of agricultural and food chemistry* 60.36 (2012): 8776-8782.

[47] Richards, James L., et al. "Dietary metabolites and the gut microbiota: an alternative approach to control inflammatory and autoimmune diseases." *Clinical & translational immunology* 5.5 (2016): e82.

[48] Badsha, Humeira. "Role of diet in influencing rheumatoid arthritis disease activity." *The open rheumatology journal* 12 (2018): 19.

[49] Barbaresko, Janett, et al. "Dietary pattern analysis and biomarkers of low-grade inflammation: a systematic literature review." *Nutrition reviews* 71.8 (2013): 511-527.

[50] Vasconcelos, Ilka M., and José Tadeu A. Oliveira. "Antinutritional properties of plant lectins." *Toxicon* 44.4 (2004): 385-403.

[51] Hamid, Rabia, and Akbar Masood. "Dietary lectins as disease causing toxicants." *Pakistan Journal of Nutrition* 8.3 (2009): 293-303.

[52] Gupta, Raj Kishor et al. "Reduction of phytic acid and enhancement of bioavailable micronutrients in food grains" *Journal of food science and technology* vol. 52,2 (2013): 676-84.

INDEX

ABOUT THE AUTHORS

Mercy Ballard, RN / Director of Years Restored Lifestyle and Learning Center. Mercy suffered many years with severe anemia, pain and fatigue, before learning about how food sensitivities and gut permeability contributed to her symptoms. Driven by her own struggles with her health, Mercy started creating the recipes which are now the basis of this cookbook. Inspired by her recovery, she set out to help others facing similar health conditions. In 2013, she and her husband moved to Central California where they began the Years Restored Lifestyle and Learning Center. Here, she provides education in nutrition, lifestyle, and natural remedies to help others with autoimmune, food sensitivities and other chronic diseases regain their health and purpose in life.

Dr. Joyce Choe, MD, MPH, is a board-certified ophthalmologist from Vancouver, WA. She is a plant-based health enthusiast who has led a wide variety of community-based health programs. Her passion is to help her patients make the paradigm shifts needed to change behaviors and to improve their quality of life. Her own health journey led to an in-depth search for answers and caused her to see the need for information and education about the growing problem of gut permeability and the amazing possibilities for improved health that a specific plant-based lifestyle can give.

Connect online

Autoimmuneplantbased.com

Yearsrestored.com

DrJoyceChoe.com

Facebook group: Plant Based Gut Health

Instagram

YouTube

Made in the USA
San Bernardino, CA
14 December 2019